Dissonance in Zion

"We live in a dissatisfied country, an unhappy country, a violent and tragically splintered country."

André Brink, *Mapmakers*

Dissonance in Zion

Michael Jansen

Zed Books Ltd.
London and New Jersey

Dissonance in Zion was first published by Zed Books Ltd.,
57 Caledonian Road, London N1 9BU, UK, and
171 First Avenue, Atlantic Highlands, New Jersey 07716,
USA, in 1987.

Cover designed by Andrew Corbett
Printed in the United Kingdom
at The Bath Press, Avon.

British Library Cataloguing in Publication Data

Jansen, Michael
  Dissonance in Zion.
  1. Israel—Politics and government
  I. Title
  320.95694   JQ1825.P3

  ISBN 0-86232-682-6
  ISBN 0-86232-683-4 Pbk

For my mother, Dorothy Ellen Wood

Contents

Acknowledgements

Because Israel is generally presented to the world as a solidly unified country, with all its component peoples successfully melted into the national pot, outsiders have little notion of the partisanship and particularism of Israeli political life. Israel is a country of opinionated people and conflicting ideologies. While gathering material for this book the author paid two visits to the country and interviewed more than fifty Israelis who spoke frankly about their society and its current political situation. The author owes a profound debt to the following:

In particular, to Aimée Ginsberg, a student of political science at the Hebrew University of Jerusalem, who helped me make appointments, translated where necessary and suggested people worth meeting.

Paul Mendesflohr, Professor of Jewish Studies at the Hebrew University, a follower of Martin Buber and author of a book on his teachings.

Raya Roten, schoolteacher and political activist: Women Against the War in Lebanon, Committee Against the War in Lebanon, Citizens Who Care.

Daniel Amit, Professor of Physics at the Hebrew University and member of the Committee for Solidarity with Birzeit and the Committee Against the War in Lebanon.

Dani Flexer, student at the Hebrew University, member of leftish CAMPUS student group.

Eli Gozansky, conscript soldier who served three terms in prison for refusing duty in Lebanon, a member of the Communist Party.

David Ist Shalom, businessman and activist on the Committee for Israel-Palestine Peace.

Yehoshafat Harkabi, Professor of Political Science at the Hebrew University, formerly chief of Military Intelligence and security adviser to the Prime Minister, regarded as Israel's foremost expert on the PLO, a 'hardline' dove.

Yehudit Blanc, member of the Committee Against the War in Lebanon.

David Shaham, executive director of the International Centre for Peace in the Middle East.

Rubin Kaminer, Dean of Overseas Students at the Hebrew University and editor of *Israleft*.

Aurora Jacob, student at the Hebrew University, member of Women

Against the War.

Yeheskel Landau, spokesman of Oz VeShalom, the religious peace group.

Alouph Hareven, head of the Education Programme at the Van Leer Jerusalem Foundation and editor of its publications.

Amiram Goldbloom, Hadassa Medical Centre School of Pharmacy, spokesman of Peace Now.

Janet Aviad, a sociologist connected with the Van Leer Institute, a Peace Now activist.

Eliesar Schweid, Professor of Jewish Studies at the Hebrew University, strong supporter of the Greater Israel ideology.

Dani Rubinstein, highly respected West Bank correspondent of the Histadrut daily, *Davar*.

Peretz Kidron, journalist.

Leah Tsemel, a lawyer who defends Palestinian detainees.

Meron Benvenisti, former Deputy Mayor of Jerusalem, head of West Bank Data Base Project.

Mordechai Bar-On, former Chief Education Officer of the Israel Army, Peace Now activist and Member of the Knesset for the Citizens' Rights Movement.

Raya Harnik, journalist, mother of an officer killed at the battle for Beaufort, peace activist.

Michael Ratson, second-in-command of the Youth Herut, adviser to Ariel Sharon, member of the Municipal Council of Rosh Ha'Ain, a development town settled by Yemenis, a reserve major in the Army.

Shlomo Elbaz, Professor of French at the Hebrew University, of Moroccan origin, founder of the Oriental 'East for Peace' movement.

B. Michael, satirist of *Ha'aretz*, bitter opponent of the Likud.

Saadia Martziano, former Member of the Knesset for the Black Panthers Party, of Moroccan origin, leader of the 'Shahak' neighbourhood movement in the Musrara Quarter of Jerusalem.

Mattityahu Peled, former Army general, Professor of Arabic at Tel Aviv University, founder of the Progressive List for Peace Party and Member of Knesset.

Mordechai Gur, former Army Chief-of-Staff, Labour Knesset Member and Minister of Health in the 1984 National Unity Government.

Israel Shahak, Professor of Biochemistry at the Hebrew University, President of the Israel League for Human and Civil Rights.

Shulamit Aloni, Knesset Member for the Citizens' Rights Movement.

Mark Heller, of the Institute for Strategic Studies at Tel Aviv University, author of *A Palestinian State*.

Mina Tsemach, Director of the Dachov Institute for Public Opinion Research, Tel Aviv.

Doron Vilner, head of the young Communists, Yesh Gvul activist.

Avraham Burg, son of the Minister of Interior and Police Yosef Burg in the second Likud Government, Peace Now activist and officer of the New Israel Fund.

Israel Eldad, former ideologist of Lehi (the Stern Gang), founder of the Tehiya Party and promoter of the policies of the militant Gush Emunim settlers' movement.

Yehuda Litani, highly respected West Bank correspondent of *Ha'aretz*.

The late Naomi Kies, Professor of Political Science at the Hebrew University, member of the Committee Against the War in Lebanon.

Ehud Olmert, Likud Knesset Member and its parliamentary spokesman.

Emanuel Halperin, Likud activist, with Jerusalem Television.

Amnon Katz, student at the Hebrew University, a reservist who refused to serve in Lebanon.

Gershon Ben Shachar, Professor of Psychology at the Hebrew University.

This book could not have been written if the Israeli press had been less rigorous in its examination of the society than it is. The author depended heavily on the excellent translations from the Hewbrew press made by the International Centre for Middle East Peace, *Israleft* and Dr Israel Shahak. *The Jerusalem Post* was particularly useful. On the military side, the work of Professor Yoram Peri, his book *Between Battles and Ballots* and articles in the international press, illuminated the role of the Israel Defence Forces in politics.

Glossary

Agudat Yisrael.	International political and religious movement, originally opposed to the State, which became one of Israel's political parties.
Alignment (Labour Alignment).	
	The alliance of the Israeli Labour Party (Mapai) and the left-wing socialist Mapam formed in 1969 and effectively dissolved in 1984.
Aliya.	Immigration to Israel.
Ashkenazim.	Jews of German and Eastern European descent.
Bar Kokhba, Shimon.	Leader of a revolt in Judea against the Roman Empire. He was killed when his last stronghold fell.
Betar.	Formerly the youth movement of the Revisionist Party, inherited by the present-day Herut Party.
Eretz Yisrael.	The Land of Israel.
Etzel.	See Irgun Zvai Leumi.
Greater Land of Israel	Movement advocating the annexation of the territories captured in the 1967 war.
Green Line.	The old armistice lines between Israel and the neighbouring Arab states, fixed in 1949.
Gush Emunim.	The militant messianic movement which seeks to extend Jewish settlement throughout the territories.
Haganah.	The semi-underground defence force of the Jewish colonists in Palestine. Transformed into the Israel Defence Forces in 1948.
Herut.	The right-wing heir of the Revisionist Party, led by Menachem Begin, which in 1973 became the leading component of the Likud bloc.
Histadrut.	Israel's general federation of labour.
Irgun Zvai Leumi (also known as Etzel).	
	Jewish underground organization active from 1937 until 1948, led by Menachem Begin for much of the time.

Jabotinsky, Vladimir.	Russian-born journalist and Zionist leader, founder of the militaristic Revisionist Party.
Likud.	Right-wing bloc formed in 1973 and headed by the Herut Party's Menachem Begin.
Mapai.	The democratic socialist Labour Party, led by Ben Gurion in the pre-state period and during the first years of the state's existence. Formed an alliance with the left-wing Mapam in 1969 known as the Labour Alignment.
Mapam.	The left-wing socialist party, was part of the Labour Alignment until 1984 when Mapai agreed to form a national unity government with the Likud.
Morasha.	An extremist offshoot of the National Religious Party.
National Religious Party.	Political Party founded in 1956, dedicated to the establishment of the rule of the Tora in Israel, and the extension of Jewish sovereignty over the entire Land of Israel.
Palmach.	Élite strike force of the Haganah from 1941 to 1948.
Peace Now.	Peace movement launched in 1978 which undertakes mass action to promote peace.
Progressive List for Peace.	New joint-Arab-Jewish list of candidates which stood in the 1984 election. Promotes the establishment of a Palestinian State in the occupied territories.
Revisionists.	Zionist party founded in 1925 by Vladimir Jabotinsky which promoted Jewish settlement on both sides of the Jordan River and advocated the use of force to solve the problems encountered by the Zionist Organization. Parent of the Herut Party.
Sephardim.	Jews of Spanish or Portuguese descent, also used to refer to the Oriental — Asian and North African — Jews.
Shas.	Oriental religious party founded in 1984.
Tami.	Oriental offshoot of the National Religious Party.
Tehiya.	The 'National Renaissance Party' opposing concessions to the Arabs.
Yamit.	Israeli town in Sinai evacuated in April 1982 under the 1979 Israel-Egypt peace treaty.

Introduction: The Importance of Dissonance

This book is meant to be a guide to the contemporary Israeli political scene, a description of where Israel has reached and how it got there, and an assessment of the possibility of peace in the region.

The book's focus is the 1982 invasion of Lebanon which was, and remains, a critical experience for Israel. This war brought to the surface of Israeli political life the ideological contradictions within the Zionist ideology of the state and deepened the socio-cultural division of the society produced by the in-gathering of Jews from the world over. This deepening rift jeopardizes the democratic foundations of the state and, because of the need for an external challenge to re-establish a national consensus, threatens to plunge the Middle East into a new war.

The Lebanon war must not, however, be regarded as an isolated experience, as a departure from the four wars that preceded it. It was an expected enterprise in the century-old struggle being waged by militant Zionists for possession of all the territory they call 'Eretz Yisrael' which had once been included in the historical Jewish kingdoms. Though Israel occupied most of the land it claimed during the 1967 war it has been unable either to gain possession of this land because of the presence and resistance of its Palestinian inhabitants or to achieve a legitimate hold because the international community remains reluctant to accept Israel's acquisition of the territory by conquest.

Thus the doubly frustrated architects of the 1982 war — Menachem Begin, Ariel Sharon and Raphael Eitan — chose to use force to break the impasse. They believed that their war would be the final battle for Eretz Yisrael. The Israeli Army would eliminate the Palestine Liberation Organization and with it destroy the rival claim to the Land of the Palestinian people. But the Lebanon war was no more than a messianic dream. The PLO acquitted itself well in the fighting, gaining new international stature, then in 1984 proposed negotiations for an Arab-Israeli settlement based on an exchange of peace for a portion of the Land, a proposition that is anathema to Zionist militants. For them the 1982 experience, in the opinion of Professor Yehoshafat Harkabi, a former director of Military Intelligence and security adviser to Prime Minister Begin, was 'a period in which God failed'. It was the first of Israel's wars which did not have a 'miraculous' result and the first which made the Israeli public see the limitations of military action. And the war earned Israel a new international reputation defined by Professor Harkabi as 'the prestige of cruelty', applying an expression used to describe the Roman Empire.

The most important result of the Lebanon war was the mass disaffection of ordinary Israelis from the policies of their government, which had heretofore been given automatic support by the vast majority at times of war. There had always been a vocal minority who had been critical of the Government, spoken out against Israel's policies towards its Arab neighbours and favoured accommodation with the Palestinians, but this minority had always been too small and too weak to do more than act as a restraining influence on the Government's militant policies. But in 1982-83 the Government found itself up against a bloc of about 25 per cent of the population who opposed the Lebanon war and demanded that Israel make the concessions necessary to achieve peace with the Arabs and coexistence with the Palestinians.

This minority of concessionist peacemakers had emerged at the time the Zionist movement was founded and produced a buzzing dissonance within Zionism throughout the pre-state period and during the first 20 years of the history of the state. After the conquests of 1967 this buzzing became an ever increasing juddering in the mechanism of the Zionist movement; after 1982 the dissonance became a shuddering throb accompanied by a note of warning. Israelis who had previously considered only what *they* wanted, who believed that *they* could achieve anything if *they* willed it and were prepared to sacrifice for it, began to see that the rival point of view had to be taken into account, that there had to be reciprocity before there could be accommodation. In 1982 dissonance became a potentially revolutionary force in Zion, and the only chance for peace in the Middle East. But it has also produced a violent reaction among the most militant sections of the population — those who would rather fight than talk — and has deepened and broadened the existing rift in Israeli society which threatens not only the unity of the country but also of the Zionist movement.

1. Dissonance in Zion

Two Marches

The setting sun had shut down the Sabbath. From Galilee to the Negev, from the coastal cities and silent kibbutzim, people were on the move, in buses and cars, coming to Jerusalem. In the city itself others put on sturdy shoes, heavy sweaters and warm hats, and set out for Zion Square. Jaffa Road was dark, deserted, the shops shuttered: the bright beacon that drew us towards the Square was a petromax lamp at a fruit stall huddled in an alley just before the corner. Ben Yehuda Street beyond blossomed with light. A few hundred people stood about in bunches, friends foregathering. Not the 25,000 expected. But it was early. We too searched for congenial companions. Organizers of the march, and of the various groups taking part, distributed homemade torches, to be fired when we approached the Prime Minister's office. Others handed round placards on poles, the Hebrew words demanding, 'Get Out of Lebanon', 'Stop the Settlements', 'End the Occupation'; proclaiming, 'Enough!' 'There is a Limit!' A tall man in a wool plaid jacket took several and bore them off to his group: 'We can use the sticks to defend ourselves if we're attacked again.' Violence might come later; there would be none in this place: the army and police were almost as numerous as marchers, ranged along the edge of the street, blocking access to Ben Yehuda from all the side-streets, above us on balconies and rooftops, light glinting on the snub barrels of sub-machine-guns, voices crackling over walkie-talkies.

Among us circulated our own *force de frappe*, off-duty reservists, a few swinging truncheons or leaning on staves. A third khaki force collected in the Square, the men who had refused to serve in Lebanon, and had gone to gaol serving their principles instead. Buses freed their passengers on Jaffa Road and Ben Yehuda filled with marchers. Small children rode on their fathers' shoulders. Elderly couples gathered under a small tree exclaiming in surprise over how many of their friends they had seen (for only troublemakers demonstrated!) There were many men wearing crocheted skull caps or *kippas*, usually the emblem of the violent right; these were members of the religious peace groups. Absent were the very young in great numbers — those of conscript age who led the anti-war protest in the United States. The majority were between 25 and 40, quiet, polite, well-dressed, a solid chunk of the

1

political centre. A visiting founder-member of the American Communist Party, a vigorous 80-year-old, eyes sparkling above a full white beard, reviewed this curious peace rally, inspired by the committed centre, with the left as fellow-travellers, all operating under agreed non-partisan slogans. Weaving through the growing crowd were Palestinians from Umm el-Fahm, the largest Arab town in Israel, Palestinians anxious that this demonstration might succeed.

Marchers squeezed into the corridor of Ben Yehuda from Bezalel Street at the top and Zion Square at the bottom until we were packed together, compressed, then we moved, in a body, a serpent or dragon, perhaps, torch flames its glinting scales, slipping through the confines of Ben Yehuda, over the cobbled roadbed, into the open and vulnerable streets watched over by armed troops and police, through the empty city. Soldiers on the Bezalel overpass leaned over the rail to see us march beneath, twenty people abreast. A few observers gathered behind police barriers in the Oriental Nahalot neighbourhood silently surveyed the procession. A small, crabbed man in dark clothing scurried along the pavement shouting insults: 'Beautiful Souls!' 'Traitors!', before ducking into a side-street. Protests against protests were no longer fashionable. We flowed along one lane of the dual carriageway, into the plaza before the Prime Minister's office building, curled round it and overflowed up the grassy slopes of the park. The speeches had begun, out of sight round the corner, but the broadcast words were clear and uncompromising. The first speech demanded withdrawal from Lebanon and an end to the concentration of resources in the territories occupied since 1967, the second called for a new alliance between the Oriental poor and liberal intellectuals, the third warned against the rise of the violent political right and the fourth, by Jerusalem's mayor, had as its theme the 'terrorism from within' which could undermine and bring about the disintegration of Israeli society. The Israeli national anthem was sung. Then the mass left, as silently, as modestly as they had come, in buses, in cars, on foot through the cold, dark February night, torches snuffed out, placards lowered. Fifty thousand people had marched, twice as many as expected, in this, Jerusalem's largest demonstration, held on the anniversary of another, tragic march.[1]

That one had been held on a Thursday, 10 February 1983, three days after a commission of inquiry had submitted its assessment of Israeli involvement in the September 1982 massacre of civilians in the Sabra–Chatila suburbs of Beirut. The Minister of Defence, Ariel Sharon, censured in the report, had refused to accept the findings of the commission and resign; the Government dithered until its critics had decided to force its hand by taking to the streets. They fixed the route from Zion Square to the Prime Minister's office that we followed a year later. But the experience of these marchers was very different from ours.

From the start they were surrounded and attacked by organized violent hooligans. 'Begin. Begin. Begin. PLO-PLO-PLO-PLO. Arik, King of Israel. Arik, King of Israel. It won't do you any good, you PLO supporters, you're trash. Your commission is rubbish. How dare you set up a commission against Arik, against Begin. We're going to kill you, do a Sabra and Chatila to you, a holocaust ... You're trash, trash, trash!' The marchers were few, perhaps 1,500 began the walk from Zion Square. The police were neither prepared for what happened nor ready to intervene. The Government's supporters burst into the procession, shouting, punching the marchers, spitting in their faces, using sexual invective, calling even the Army reservists among them 'traitors', 'PLO'. The marchers did not react, did not fight back. A few hurried away to telephone for reinforcements, and rejoined the procession. Which became 2,000. The thugs threw burning cigarettes into the faces of the demonstrators, one tried to hold a burning torch before the eyes of a woman artist from the Israel museum. Many of the opposition wore the knitted *kippas* of the religious right, others identified themselves as Oriental Jews, the underprivileged who loved Begin. A 16-year-old boy who had joined the peace march was set upon and his shirt was torn. They attacked a veteran of the Entebbe raid. 'Have you been in the Army? You PLO supporter.' At the front of the march six reserve paratroopers linked arms to form a human wall, to force a way among rows of these violent men. A former Haganah member was kicked while passing the place where she helped bandage people wounded in a car bomb explosion 35 years before: 'Was it for this that we fought for a state?'

The square at the end of Ben Yehuda Street was filled with Rabbi Kahane's men. Borne high on the shoulders of a supporter the Rabbi shouted that the demonstrators were all 'traitors', their cause 'a knife in the back of the nation'. Kahane's American vigilantes began punching an elderly couple, survivors of the Holocaust. Schoolgirls were drenched in spit. The procession was halted at the Bezalel bridge, where stones rained down from above. The marchers pressed on, 3,000 strong. They lit their torches. Outside the Prime Minister's office they collected in the parking lot, where a large force of police and frontier troops restrained the supporters of Begin and Sharon who had taken over the slopes commanding the area where the marchers had gathered. Inside the Cabinet was in session. Outside 'Arik, Arik, Arik. Begin, Begin, Begin!' drowned out the speakers, including a professor from the religious university when he read a verse from the Bible. The marchers sang Hatikva and dispersed. A group of young men standing on the slope watched attentively. 'Now!' came a call, then a shattering explosion. Emil Grunsweig, one of the paratroopers who had led the procession, a reservist who had returned from duty in Lebanon only a few days before, lay dying on the pavement, shrapnel from an army-issue grenade penetrating his chest just above his heart. The other wounded were taken away in cars and at the entrance to the emergency ward of the hospital a doctor and a demonstrator were attacked by thugs who had followed them. 'Begin, Begin, Begin! Arik, Arik, Arik!' The earlier demonstration had brought a taste of civil war to the streets of Jerusalem; the latter showed just how afraid the authorities were of internal conflict; the two revealed the extent to which Israeli society had been polarized between two ideological orientations, those of the small Israel and the greater Israel. Although none of the founders of the Jewish state could have imagined that 35 years after its founding its people could be so deeply divided, such polarization was inevitable, given the ideological divisions that always existed within Zionism,

3

the ethnic and social mix of the Israeli population, and the militant character of the state. Chapter 1 will deal with the first two reasons for this polarization and Chapters 2 and 3 with the third.

The Four Schools of Thought

The Zionist movement was, from its founding, a strategic alliance formed by a multitude of parties and factions whose sole common idea was the promotion of Jewish settlement in Palestine. The groups even disagreed about the objective of the organization they founded: the establishment of a Jewish state. There were 'General' (liberal, anti-religious), 'Catastrophic' (refusing to accept that Jews should continue to dwell in the Diaspora after the founding of the state), 'Evolutionary', 'Revolutionary', 'Pragmatic', 'Romantic' 'Cultural', 'Political', 'Messianic', 'Democratic', 'Liberal' and 'Revisionist' Zionists, to name a few. By the time the state was founded in 1948 the multiplicity of ideological factions had coalesced into four distinct ideological schools of thought and action, which have survived until today.

The *first* ideology was messianic. It emerged as a revival of millennial Jewish messianism in reaction to the opening up of Gentile European society to Jews following the French Revolution of 1789. The traditional-minded recoiled from emancipation and assimilation by reasserting the necessity to return to communal solidarity and exclusiveness, without which, they argued, Judaism would not survive and the Jewish people would lose their distinctiveness. Although the original messianics rejected immigration to Palestine because they believed that the Jewish people could only be reconstituted in Eretz Yisrael through the agency of God at a time chosen by Him, some made their way to Palestine, settled there to await developments promised in the scriptures and came to believe that their participation in the establishment of a Jewish state in Zion (Palestine) was necessary for Jewish redemption and the fulfilment of the prophecies concerning the advent of the Messiah. The man who both promoted the cause of Zionism among the Orthodox in the Diaspora and created a role for the Orthodox in Palestine was Rabbi Yitzak Hacohen Kook. Kook, who settled in Jaffa in 1904, was a mystic and a religious Zionist preoccupied with preparations for the 'end of days'. In the pre-state period he urged tolerance among all the builders of the modern state—secularists and heretics included—and made himself ready to assume the office of high priest in a restored Temple in Jerusalem.

Kook elevated the Land, Eretz Yisrael, to the position of supreme importance in the process of the redemption of the Jewish people:

> Eretz Yisrael is not something apart from the soul of the Jewish people; it is no mere national possession, serving as a means of unifying our people and buttressing its material, or even its spiritual survival. Eretz Yisrael is part of the very essence of our nationhood; it is bound organically to its very life and inner being . . . Jewish original creativity, whether in the realm of ideas or in the arena of daily life and action, is impossible except in Eretz Yisrael...A Jew

cannot be as devoted and true to his own ideas, sentiments, and imagination in the Diaspora as he can in Eretz Yisrael.[2]

It was natural for Kook to stress the pre-eminence of the Land among the three traditional components of Judaism—Land, Tora and People: the Jews, who had been despised for millennia because of their homelessness, required Land to re-establish themselves as a people and resume living according to the prescriptions of the Tora. As a practical man he could not ignore the predominance of the secularists in the Zionist enterprise, nor the fact that the entire Jewish people was not moved to settle in Eretz Yisrael. But he believed that once the Land was secured, Jewish unity and the rule of the Tora must follow.

Although Rabbi Yitzak Hacohen Kook was the chief conciliator of his day, his teachings, as interpreted by his son, Rabbi Zvi Kook, became doctrines that have divided Israel. These were described by Amos Elon, one of Israel's foremost writers, as '"messianism" and divinification of the Land, sanctification of violence and a mystification of force'. The younger Kook set the tone: 'In Merkaz Harav yeshiva in Jerusalem' Kook

> raised a generation of zealots, 'a new Jewish man', as Haim Be'er [who knew Kook] put it, 'a Savonarola in a knitted skullcap, wrapped in a prayer shawl and armed with a Kalashnikov; nationalistic, callously trampling down the water-melon beds of the Arabs of Samaria and uprooting the vineyards of Hebron', all the while trailing clouds of purity and specious words . . . 'like the Ayatollah Khomeini, he flourished near the end of his days, in a dark and frightening efflorescence . . . An ascetic, lacking all self-restraint . . . Exerting a magus-like influence over his faithful disciples'[3]

. . .of both the secular and religious messianic camps, particularly Gush Emunim. For such people, Bar Ilan University Professor Uriel Simon says, there is 'a romantic appeal to the psychological and spiritual capability of defying reality . . . It contains the illusion of a revival of the pioneering days of Zionism' which they missed. These new messianics 'regard themselves as having a kind of divine insurance policy releasing them from any moral constraints'.[4]

The *second* surviving ideology emerged at about the same time as the messianic. It also involved messianism, but of a liberal enlightened kind. This was 'spiritual' Zionism. Its adherents, both religious and secular, believed that the Jewish people's fate was to be dispersed and their mission was to transmit their unique spiritual genius to the societies in which they lived. The spiritual Zionists gave precedence to the Book, The Tora, and set out to establish in Palestine a Jewish community of exceptional moral character which could serve as a spiritual centre for the Jews of the Diaspora comparable to that established at Jamnia by the quietist Rabbi Johanan ben Zakkia after the Romans defeated the Jewish rebellion under Bar Kokhba in 136 AD and the Jews of Judea were dispersed. The most influential exponent of this ideology was Ahad HaAm (Asher Ginsberg) who believed that the Jews' special contribution was that 'at a very early period' the Prophets had taught the

Jewish people to 'respect the power of the spirit and not to worship material power'. Ahad HaAm said that the Jews had survived because of their 'nationalism of spirit' as opposed to the nationalism of the sword practised by the rest of humanity.

But the intolerance displayed by the new European romantic nationalisms— with their emphasis on the particularity of each *folk*—disillusioned the spiritual Zionists. They too came to believe that at least a partial solution to the problem of anti-semitism lay in the settlement of Jews in Palestine. This shift to the Palestine solution did not cause them to lose their humanity: they alone among the settlers were able to empathize with the Palestinian Arabs and understand their objections to a Zionist takeover of the country. The spiritual Zionists tried to promote cooperation between immigrants and the indigenous people. Ahad HaAm paid a visit to Palestine soon after the Zionist colonization effort began and was compelled to write in 1891 that the Jewish colonists 'treat the Arabs with hostility and cruelty, deprive them of their rights, offend them without cause and even boast of their deeds; and nobody among us opposes this despicable and dangerous inclination'. Like the messianic Kook, the spiritual Ahad HaAm also immigrated to Palestine, settling there in 1921, where, alarmed by the confrontation brewing between the settlers and the indigenous people, he wrote:

> Is *this* the dream of a return to Zion which our people have dreamt for centuries: that we now come to Zion to stain its soil with blood? . . . Are we really [returning to Zion] only to add in an Oriental corner a small people of new Levantines who vie with other Levantines in shedding blood, in desire for vengeance and in angry violence?[5]

Several of the more distinguished colonists from the first *aliyah*, immigration to Palestine, agreed with Ahad HaAm's criticism of fellow settlers. In 1907 Dr Yitzak Epstein, one of the more influential of these critics, attempted to warn fellow Zionists about the

> . . . Question of our relations with the Arabs. Our own national aspirations depend upon the correct solution of this question. It has not been eliminated. It simply has been forgotten by the Zionists and is hardly referred to at all in its true form in Zionist literature.[6]

The spiritual Zionists took up the banner of true moderation. In the late 1920s they organized the Brit Shalom (Covenant of Peace) group which called for restricted immigration and a negotiated settlement with the Arabs. The key official figure to promote this line was Chaim Arlosoroff, appointed head of the Jewish Agency's political department in 1931 (becoming, in effect, the Prime Minister of the Jewish community in Palestine). With the acquiescence of the Zionist Executive, Arlosoroff engaged in talks with various Arab leaders and had some success in convincing them that the Zionists would put forward a plan for cooperation between Arabs and Jews. In 1933, while laying the ground for such a plan, Arlosoroff was assassinated. The extremist Zionist faction which followed the fourth of the ideologies to be discussed— Revisionism—was believed to be responsible. But it is doubtful whether Arlosoroff would have been permitted by the Zionist Executive to develop his proposals beyond the planning stage because the Executive never wavered from its demand for a Jewish state in the whole of Palestine.

In 1936 Brit Shalom, reconstituted as the Ihud Group with such members as Dr Judah Magnes, the founder of the Hebrew University of Jerusalem, and the philosopher Martin Buber, put forward a proposal for a binational accord. This was summarily dismissed by the Executive, which opted for the British plan for partition of the country. In 1948, after the establishment of the state in 82 per cent of Palestine and the expulsion of the bulk of the Palestinian Arab population, the Ihud Group dropped the binational idea, but the Group still remained a force in both Israel and liberal circles abroad.

Israel's admirers and Israeli humanists considered that Israel must not be a 'nation like other nations' but a nation with a spiritual quality that elevated it above others; as a moral beacon Israel had a greater claim on the world's sympathy, and resources, than other new nations. Then in 1967 Israel itself placed in jeopardy this special position by occupying the remaining 18 per cent of Palestine and the Syrian Golan Heights and Egyptian Sinai. The spiritual Zionists were alarmed by this occupation, and by the consolidation of Israel's hold on the territories, because they feared their annexation and absorption of the Palestinians living in them would create a binational state in which the Palestinians would be oppressed. The spiritual Zionists adopted the line that Palestine should be 'repartitioned', that the territory taken in 1967 should be traded for peace with the Arab world. This was a radical departure from the traditional Zionist position that Jewish sovereignty should be extended over the whole of Eretz Yisrael. Present-day spiritual, or 'neo-spiritual', Zionists have refocused on the ideology of Ahad HaAm, particularly on his contention that the moral and ethical quality of the Jewish entity should be of paramount importance. The neo-spiritualists' campaign for a 'small, more Jewish Israel' runs counter to the programme of ingesting the occupied territories that is being implemented by the Israeli Government and the Jewish Agency, under strong pressure from the messianics and the followers of the fourth ideology, Revisionism.

The *third* ideology to survive was democratic socialism as represented by Labour Zionism, which emerged alongside revolutionary communism, socialism and anarchism in Europe during the last half of the 19th century. The Labour Zionists concentrated on the Jewish people. They sought to liberate the Jewish masses, particularly those in Eastern Europe and Russia, from both capitalist exploitation and anti-semitic persecution. Like the spiritual Zionists, the Labour Zionists were at first liberal and internationalist in their outlook, believing that Jewish labour should be integrated with the organized labour movements in Europe. But the 1881-82 Russian pogroms made the Labour Zionists switch to the Palestine solution for the Jewish masses. This tallied with the ideas of Theodore Herzl, a Vienna-educated liberal journalist, and his middle-class colleagues who had been influenced by both the pogroms and, more especially, by the Dreyfus Affair in France in 1894-95, which drove Herzl to write his political pamphlet *Der Judenstaat, The State of the Jews*, in 1895-96, and to call the First Zionist Congress at Basle in 1897.[7]

The founding Zionist Congress adopted Herzl's plan of action for achieving this state—to secure 'by public law . . . a home in Palestine'. This was to be accomplished by appealing to European princes and imperialist statesmen to use their good offices with the Ottoman Sultan to persuade him to grant a 'charter' for the Zionist colonization of Palestine. But, although Herzl insisted that the Organization must have its 'charter' before going ahead with energetic settlement activity, the momentum the movement generated propelled the Organization into undertakings considered unwise by conservatives like Herzl. When the Second Congress met in 1898 the Organization established the 'Jewish Colonial Trust' to arrange for colonization and assist Jewish migration to Palestine: 'practical' work could no longer await 'political' developments. (In time the creation of physical facts to force political developments became the *modus operandi* of the Organization, and the state it founded.)

The other task the Second Congress set for itself transformed the liberal, middle-class organization Herzl had established into the militant populist movement which captured the country. This task was designated as 'the conquest of the communities'. It involved a takeover of the leadership of Diaspora organizations from the assimilationists. The main target of this 'conquest' was the 5-million-strong Russian community, in which the majority of Zionists were members of one or other leftist party which, reversing the operation, captured the Zionist Organization itself from within. The representatives of these workers' parties attended the Congresses in ever increasing numbers, secured places on important committees and promoted projects for the creation of socialist pioneering settlements (kibbutzim), of embryonic military groupings (which became the Haganah, the pre-state armed forces) and of a general trade union (the Histadrut). On these three pillars—the kibbutzim, the Haganah and the Histadrut—Labour Zionism built the power base enabling it, eventually, to rule the new state.

Labour Zionism was not, however, a unified camp, but was fractured into several competing Marxist and socialist parties, the largest being the moderate democratic socialist Mapai of David Ben Gurion, which, in the first 29 years of the state, elected the largest number of members to the Israeli Knesset without ever gaining an absolute majority. In 1969 Mapai merged with the much smaller left-wing Mapam to form the Labour Alignment; and in 1984 Mapam seceded from the alliance. (In this book the term used for the general ideological orientation is 'Labour' while the parties will be called by their names.)

The *fourth* secular Greater Israel ideology emerged due to a dispute over tactics, but was not purely a product of that disagreement. It involved a clash of personalities and style of leadership; it resulted in the formation of a party which attracted a different following to that of Labour, the artisan and lower middle classes. The dispute arose in 1922 when, in response to Arab pressure, Britain reneged on its Balfour Declaration commitment that 'the field in which the Jewish National Home was to be established. . .was to be *the whole* of Palestine including Transjordan'. The Zionist Executive—dominated by Chaim Weizmann and David Ben Gurion—accepted this and subsequent

British decisions to restrict and circumscribe Zionist activity and ambitions, as temporary setbacks, as deviations on the road to establishing a Jewish state in all the territory promised. But this deviation set these *tactical* 'moderates' against Vladimir Jabotinsky, a populist-style leader, and his following who insisted on the right of Jews to settle in all of the territory of the mandate (a demand made by the heirs of the Jabotinskites today).

In 1929 the split between the Jabotinskites and the others intensified when Britain placed restrictions on Jewish immigration. The militant Jabotinskites called for 'revision' of the programme adopted by the Congresses, which gave them the name, 'Revisionists'. The Revisionists demanded that the Jewish Agency should *declare officially* that their objective was the creation of a *state* and oppose Britain by force of arms. Until then the words used to describe the entity the Zionists were working to establish were 'National Home' and 'home', in order to minimize Arab opposition to an independent Jewish state in their midst. The Revisionists took upon themselves the task of preventing any deviation from the original goal of a state in all of Eretz Yisrael. They were charged with the murder of Arlosoroff in 1933 because they opposed the adoption of his plan for cooperation with the Arabs; they formed an underground guerrilla group which undertook acts of terrorism, first against the British, then the Palestinians, and organized illegal immigration. In 1937, before the 20th Zionist Congress, Ben Gurion, then Arlosoroff's successor as head of the political department of the Jewish Agency, clearly stated the position of the Executive in a bid to heal the split in the movement: 'The debate has not been for or against the indivisibility of the Land of Israel. *No Zionist can forgo the smallest portion of the Land of Israel.* The Debate concerned which of the two routes would lead quicker to this common goal. [my italics]' Ben Gurion was unsuccessful. In 1947 when the United Nations proposed its partition plan, which gave the Zionists 55 per cent of the country, the majority accepted and the minority Revisionists raged. But the fact that the pre-state army, the Haganah, secured 82 per cent of Palestine for the Jewish state satisfied Israeli public opinion until the occupation in 1967 of the remaining 18 per cent renewed the general demand for annexation of this land and gave the heirs of the Revisionists, the Herut Party and later the Herut-led Likud coalition, an issue on which to build a popular political base.

The Influence of Immigration on Ideology

Of course the political weight of the ideological schools depended on the relative sizes of their constituencies in Palestine and later Israel. And the character of these constituencies changed drastically with every wave of immigrants. The colonists of the first *Aliya*, 1882–1905, were cultural and spiritual Zionists, of above-average education, who established true colonial settlements where the Palestinians were employed as labourers. But those of the second *aliya*, 1906–14, had no more than a primary education, and, because of their socialist ideological commitment, worked at the most menial jobs, keeping close to the soil and displacing some of the Arab labour. They wandered from one colony to another, creating small leftist political factions and gaining the reputation of being dangerous vagabonds. The third *aliya*, 1919–24, brought the pioneer settlers from Eastern Europe who were profoundly anti-authoritarian. They established themselves in voluntary communes and collectives, the majority affiliated with the United Kibbutz Movement. Amos Elon, the Israeli novelist, has summed up the impact of these three *aliyas*: 'They set a pattern of politics and society, of habits, passions and prejudices, that add up to what one basically calls national character.'[8] Although the national character of the Yishuv (the community of settlers), then Israel, was fixed on this European base during this period, in 1923 the Jewish Agency opened the door to 'all Jews who are willing to assist in the establishment of the Jewish National Home', thus providing other types of immigrants who would challenge the second/third *aliya* model. The 1923 legislation was particularly striking in this regard because it was meant to include the non-Zionist religious Jews, such as the Ultra-orthodox—like the Agudat Yisrael—who considered a state created by such a political organization as anathema. The immigrants who came after 1929 were mostly lower- and middle-class tradesmen and artisans, many of whom had been ruined by the economic collapse. They settled in the towns, particularly Tel Aviv, reacting against the working-class socialism and agrarian communism of the previous two waves to become capitalistic liberals and populist Revisionists. But the Zionist Organization and the Yishuv continued to be dominated by the secular moderate democratic socialists of Mapai; the population of the Jewish state at its foundation was overwhelmingly Eastern and Central European.

The Impact of the Ideological Schools on the Political System

Towards the end of the pre-state struggle the four ideological schools came to a working arrangement which became the basis of Israel's political system. The arrangement had three parts: The first provided for the continuation of the political status quo through the adoption of proportional representation in the Knesset, Israel's parliament. The second provided for the perpetuation of the British Mandatory regime concerning public Jewish religious observance. Less than a year before the creation of the state, while a UN committee was carrying out an inquiry on the future of Palestine after the expiry of the mandate in May 1948, the Labour-dominated Zionist Executive was forced to purchase the support of the anti-Zionist Agudat Yisrael Party to prevent it from declaring its opposition to the state. The price was the 'Status Quo Agreement' which was set forth in a letter to the chief rabbi of Agudat Yisrael dated 19 June 1947, promising that 'the Jewish state when it shall be established' would keep the Sabbath, ensure the observance of dietary laws in state institutions, maintain Orthodox control over laws concerning personal status (marriage and divorce) and continue to operate four educational streams, including one Orthodox and one Ultra-orthodox. The third part of the arrangement stipulated that the character and even the boundaries of the state should remain undefined. This flowed from a controversy during a session of the Provisional Assembly on 14 May 1948, only a few hours before the British mandate was to expire and the state to be proclaimed.

A dispute arose over the wording of the new state's declaration of independence concerning the appearance of the name of God in the document and definition of the boundaries of the state. Secularists objected to the use of the word 'God' for which 'Rock of Israel' ('Tsur Yisrael') was substituted, though even then a Marxist leader objected on the ground that that formulation 'leant a religious tone to the document' which he felt amounted to a 'coercion of conscience'. The Revisionists objected to a reference to the United Nations partition plan, which meant accepting borders reducing the size of the state to one-ninth of the area on both sides of the Jordan River claimed by that party. This was got around by announcing before the reading of the proclamation that several signees had reservations about the text which would be discussed later in a special meeting. As a result of this experience no Israeli government has attempted further definition: thus Israel has no constitution, no bill of rights, no fixed boundaries.

By the time Israel became independent the four ideological schools had formed two political camps: three became one and one remained on its own: the spiritual and moderate messianic schools joined with the dominant democratic socialist Labour school to govern while the secular militant Revisionists stood alone and out of power (see Appendix). But this situation was not to endure because, first, the pattern of *aliya* changed, bringing in Oriental Jews from the Arab countries and changing the ethnic balance within the society; and, second, the new immigrants gradually left Labour to support the Revisionists. When the Revisionists came to power in 1977, the messianics — both moderates and militants — realigned themselves with the Revisionists, whose doctrines were closer to their own. Thus two camps remained, but with two ideological schools in each, the Revisionists and messianics against Labour and the spiritualists. Furthermore, after the return of the Revisionists to power in 1981, and the heightening of political tension in the society, the smaller, more intensely motivated ideological schools dominated the two larger components.

The Ethnic Shift Produces a Second National Character Model

Ironically, it was the Labour Governments' policy of bringing immigrants from the Middle East and North Africa to Israel in the 1950s and early 1960s that produced the ethnic and political changes in the society which brought the Revisionists to power. As a result of this immigration Israel was transformed from being a predominantly European to a majority Oriental society. Today 60 per cent of Israelis are of 'Oriental' origin (Arab, Iranian, Turkish, Kurdish, Indian), of these more than half come from Arab North

Africa, and of the Asian Jews, three-fifths come from Iraq and Yemen. These Oriental Jews are mistakenly called 'Sephardim'. The true Sephardim, the descendants of the dispersed Spanish and Portuguese Jewish community, retained their distinctive religious practices and Latin tongue and settled in Southern Europe and Turkey. The confusion between the two groups has been caused by the fact that the Oriental Jews follow religious rites very similar to those of the Sephardim and come under the jurisdiction of the Sephardi Rabbinate in Israel.

The Oriental Jews who immigrated to Israel were in the majority conservative, uneducated and religiously observant; they entered their new country at the bottom of the economic and social scale. For one generation they voted for Labour, as a gesture of thanks. But Labour failed them. They were treated as second-class citizens: they remained longer in resettlement centres than European immigrants, were generally sent to frontier areas and development towns and were given employment as agricultural and construction workers and domestic help, jobs which, after the occupation of Gaza and the West Bank in 1967, were filled by Palestinians, pushing the Oriental Jews one rung up the ladder. The Orientals were also alienated by Labour's strident secularism. They moved to the Revisionist Herut Party (or the Likud coalition led by Herut) rather than the religious parties because these parties were dominated by European Ashkenazi rabbis. (Before the 1984 election Oriental rabbis formed their own religious party, the Sephardi Tora Guardians, *Shas*, which secured four seats in the Knesset.)

To a certain extent Revisionist ideology was a substitute for the far narrower doctrine preached by the religious parties: former general and intelligence chief, now professor, Yehoshafat Harkabi said that in spite of the fact that Jabotinsky 'knew nothing of Judaism' he still 'tallied . . . with some feeling of transcendental support of the Jews'. In Revisionism, the Orientals could have messianism without religious orthodoxy. They also identified personally with Menachem Begin, who had been Israel's perennial underdog, and felt at home with his easy religious observance and practice of traditional Jewish custom. Begin's simplistic demagoguery also had a powerful appeal among Orientals. Furthermore, his Herut Party, particularly its Betar youth movement (which has a very popular football team) both recruited and promoted young Orientals.

Election results show how the Oriental vote progressively shifted away from Labour until the 1977 election when the Likud won 51 per cent of the vote. And the trend has continued: in 1981 nearly 53 per cent went to the Likud-Tehiya bloc and in 1984 this rose to 55 per cent, with a further 2.5 per cent voting for the ultra-extremist Kach Party of Rabbi Meir Kahane. During this period Labour's share of the Oriental vote fell: from 25 per cent in 1977 to 22.5 per cent in 1981 and 23 per cent in 1984, adding the votes of Labour's post-election ally the newly formed Yahad Party of former Likud Defence Minister Ezer Weizman. Roughly speaking, 70–75 per cent of the Likud's supporters and 25–30 per cent of Labour's supporters are Oriental. And, the Oriental population is growing at a faster rate than the European.[9]

Because of this ethnic shift the Jewish state did not emerge as a totally representative demographic cross-section of World Jewry: the 2 million Oriental Jews who comprise only one-sixth or one-seventh of the entire Jewish people have almost all been concentrated in Israel. This lopsided demographic pattern not only changed the political balance between Israel's parties, and their ideological schools, but also, and more importantly, altered the political character of the state. According to David Landau, the diplomatic correspondent of *The Jerusalem Post*, if Israel had been a cross-section of the Jewish people, the democratic values of religious pluralism, liberalism and respect for the opinions of others would have continued to prevail, but the Oriental *aliya* changed the political and social values of the society.[10]

The majority of young Israelis (aged 18-22) are no longer pioneering leftists but are increasingly right-wing in their views. According to the distinguished Israeli sociologist and military historian, Yoram Peri, 'every Jewish generation born in Greater Israel becomes more and more South African' in its attitudes. Citing an opinion poll taken during the summer of 1984, Peri says that the opinions of the Israeli Jewish public concerning the Palestinian population of the occupied territories 'should alarm anyone who still has any humane feelings left'. Fifteen per cent said that the Palestinians should be deported; 43.5 per cent said that they should be allowed to remain, but without any civil and political rights; 15 per cent said they should have equal rights, and 26 per cent said they should have self-determination. The survey projected that 60 per cent of the urban Jewish population favours a solution to the problem of the Palestinian minority involving deportation or apartheid: only one out of ten favouring deportation was an adult, while *three out of four in the 18-22 age group* supported this solution.[11] A teacher in a religious highschool in Jerusalem said that her 17-year-old students were divided between the 'Left' of Tehiya (a rightist offshoot of the Revisionist Party) and the 'Right' of Kach.

Current immigration consists of predominantly conservative, observant Jews from the United States, Russia, Western Europe and Latin America, all of whom are supporters of religious or right-wing extreme nationalist parties.

The Two Cultures

The reduction of the four ideological schools to two equal competing political camps is particularly dangerous for the society because this faultline falls along the faultline which divides the educated, secular, European 'haves' from the uneducated, observant, Oriental 'have-nots'. Thus between the two camps there are differences in culture, religion, race and economics as well as politics. During the seven years of Likud rule (1977-84) the gulf between the two camps widened because of the economic crisis brought on by uncontrolled private and public spending. The well-off were able to absorb much of the inflationary shock but the poor were not and their situation was made worse by drastic cuts in public services such as health, education and welfare. Repression in the territories and the war in Lebanon sharpened the political differences between the two camps, driving their supporters towards their respective spiritual and messianic poles. Indeed, it was the messianic militants who set Government policy.

These 'camps' have been characterized by Meron Benvenisti, former Deputy Mayor of Jerusalem, as 'political cultures'. One culture is 'moderate and liberal'; 'it stands for territorial compromise and a freeze on settlement in the occupied areas, it avoids extreme religious and historical claims and is concerned about the long-term moral damage [to Israel] caused by [its] domination of 1.3 million Palestinians' in the territories. 'The other . . . is thought to be extremist and fundamentalist; it calls for total annexation of the West Bank and Gaza and the spread of settlements in the heavily populated areas of the territories.' [12] The two cultures also hold opposing views over the future of Israel's political system. Supporters of the first culture argue that retention of the territories would mean that Israel would either have to integrate the Palestinians living there, diluting the Jewish character of their state (by 40 per cent, counting the Palestinians who are Israeli citizens from inside the 1967 borders, known as the 'Green Line') or relegate them to the sort of Bantustan existence imposed by whites on blacks in South Africa, negating Israeli democracy. The militants of the second culture insist that the integrity of Eretz Yisrael should take precedence over everything else, that retention of the Land is more important than preserving Israel's present political system: they are prepared to pay the political, social, economic and military price of continuing the occupation and suppression of the Palestinians, and, as the 1984 poll showed, they are ready, if necessary or the opportunity arises, to expel the Palestinians.

The militant mainly Ashkenazi messianics, who follow the doctrine of Rabbi Kook, have been able to capture a large proportion of the Orientals because they share the same attitude towards the Land. Oriental Zionism was not rooted in anti-semitism as was that of the Ashkenazi Zionists of Eastern and Central Europe; for the Orientals the attraction was the Land—Zion was a piece of religio-historical property which belonged to them. As such they would make no compromises, particularly with the Arabs whose countries they left for Israel. Many, even most, countries of the world are also divided into political cultures, sometimes more than two; but Israel is unique because the two cultures bisect the society and because the members of the two cultures retain their ethnic pasts, because they remain at heart Russians and Poles and Ukrainians or Yemenis and Moroccans and Kurds. Indeed, in Israel the secondary Oriental culture has a numerical edge on the prevailing predominantly Western culture—which is not true anywhere else. The results of the last three elections show that the two cultures are more or less in political equilibrium, an equilibrium which has been reinforced by the indecisive 1984 election. Though the first political culture is said to be represented by the Labour Party and the second by the Likud, Benvenisti admits that the effective difference between the political programmes of the two parties 'is negligible'. Which is why Labour and Likud politicians were able to form a national unity government after the indecisive election of 1984. Though this gap between politicians is narrow enough for them to work together within a coalition, the followers of the two camps are divided by a chasm so wide that they refuse to speak to each other, and even are unwilling to live together in the same neighbourhoods.

This is because religion has become the dominant difference between the two camps (see Appendix). Since the beginning of the Zionist enterprise in Palestine there has been friction between the religious and secular sections of the society but this has, in recent years, been transformed into a *kulturkampf*, as the Orientals have discarded, one by one, socialism, westernization and reliance on democracy, and have reverted to the comfortable social conservatism and religious orthodoxy of their former Diaspora lives, boosting the power of the Orthodox establishment and the secular and messianic militants, and encouraging authoritarianism.

This association between Orientals and Orthodox served to increase the gap between these two groups and the Western secular portion of the population, 60 per cent of whom describe the Orthodox unfavourably and only 19 per cent favourably.[13] Indeed relations between the secular and the Orthodox have deteriorated to the point that education officials have felt compelled to organize encounter sessions to bring together the youth of the two groups (as they do for Arabs and Jews). And, according to a newsletter published by a concerned group of religious educators (*Tora Va'avoda*) the chasm between the two cultures threatens to precipitate civil war between them and poses a greater danger than any external threat.

The Clash of Cultures

Ever since the first Likud government was installed in 1977, violence has been on the increase: first, in the occupied territories — between the Palestinians and the Army and the Palestinians and the settlers — then after 1981, when the second Begin government was established, the men of violence 'crossed the Green Line' from the territories into Israel proper. The 1977 election campaign was characterized by a great deal of violence; the 1981 campaign even more so, Likud supporters breaking up election meetings of Labour candidates, assaulting those attending. The 1984 campaign was less violent, because of the murder of Emil Grunsweig at the 1983 peace march. President Chaim Herzog, in his inaugural address in the first week of May 1983, said that physical and verbal violence, intolerance, fanaticism and the repudiation of democratic values may prove more dangerous than the threat from Israel's Arab enemies. He pledged himself to do battle with 'the enemy that threatens to divide us':

> This real enemy . . . is within us. It exists within every one of us citizens of Israel — Jews and Arabs, religious and secular, right-wing and left-wing, Sephardim and Ashkenazim. It is expressed in the lack of readiness to hear one's fellow man . . . when we don't agree with him.[14]

15

Herzog's motive for making such a speech was to seize the initiative from the Likud leaders who had indulged in a campaign of verbal violence against all their antagonists, Israelis as well as Palestinians. [15] Former Prime Minister Begin, while in office, referred to Palestinian guerrillas as 'two-legged animals' after the PLO withdrawal from Beirut; Army Chief of Staff Raphael Eitan spoke of the Palestinian civilians in the West bank as being 'drugged cockroaches in a bottle'; former Commander of the Northern Front General Avigdor Ben Gal described the 'Arabs' in Israel as 'a cancer in the Israeli body politic'; settlers say that 'the Arab appreciates force' and translate this into a shoot-to-kill policy in the territories. One of the favourite slogans of the extremists is 'Arabs Out!', an exact adaptation of 'Juden Raus' which was so popular in the empire of the Third Reich. For such people it is an easy step to call their countrymen, who are too 'soft' on 'Arabs', 'traitors', 'PLO' and 'beautiful souls'.

The campaign of political verbal violence and intimidation reached a peak in February 1983 over the recommendations of the Kahan commission inquiring into Israeli responsibility for the Sabra-Chatila massacre. Emil Grunsweig was the victim of this campaign. But his death made the Likud government tone down its attacks on its critics and ensure them effective police protection during demonstrations. Israel drew back from the brink of civil war, but violence still simmers just below the surface of the society.

The *kulturkampf* goes beyond disagreement over the future of the occupied territories. There is a long-standing controversy over 'who is a Jew', the Orthodox demanding that they should be the ones to decide. Liberals declare that Jews belonging to all streams of Judaism are Jews while the strict constructionist Orthodox say that only people born of a Jewish mother or converted according to Jewish Law ('Halacha') are Jews and should be accepted into the Jewish state. The first culture strives to integrate Israel's schools — religious and state — while the second holds back from integration and tries to impose its will on the state schools where children from religious homes are in a majority. The religious authorities who dominate the second culture oppose the introduction of Summer Time because they claim it would cause problems over determining the Sabbath; they are against autopsies, skin and organ banks and abortion; they resist the teaching of evolutionary theory in the schools; they try to halt archaeological digs on sites where there were or *might have been* Jewish cemeteries; they insist on general public observance of the Sabbath and fast days, including a ban on travel.

Certain very observant factions of the second culture want nothing to do with the first, or even those who are different from them within their own culture: they retreat into ghettos — certain quarters of Jerusalem, a newly constructed Ultra-orthodox urban settlement called 'Emanuel', and Orthodox Gush Emunim settlements in the West Bank. Militants from the second culture have even made guerrilla raids into the life of the first: in June 1983 a group of students from Mercaz Harav Kook disrupted a concert in Jerusalem featuring Handel's 'Messiah'; about the same time, the city's liberal mayor Teddy Kollek, was attacked by a European-origin group of Ultra-orthodox

Jews outside a synagogue where he had gone to address the congregation on the subject of tensions between the Ultra-orthodox and less observant Jews; in March 1984 two Ultra-orthodox men removed the body of a Christian-born woman, who had been married to an Israeli (and had accompanied him to a concentration camp during the Nazi period), from a Jewish cemetery in Rishon Lezion and dumped it into a nearby Muslim cemetery; in August 1984 Mayor Kollek was attacked verbally by religious spokesmen for dining in a restaurant on a fast day; and in 1984 and 1985 there were repeated Orthodox attacks on Bank Leumi, which had invested in a development scheme opposed by certain rabbis. Ultra-orthodox militants have put to the torch businesses and homes of secular and even moderately Orthodox inhabitants on the fringes of Ultra-orthodox quarters. There has been violence against Gentile places of worship and two Russian nuns living in the Ein Karem suburb of Jerusalem were murdered. And there has been strong Orthodox pressure against the completion of an American Mormon university in Jerusalem.

In the first culture a backlash is developing against the excesses of the second: youths in Jerusalem's Mekor Baruch neighbourhood have drawn up a strategy for a city-wide battle against the Ultra-orthodox campaign to close down the entire city on the Sabbath. In the Lower Galilee hamlet of Yavne'el, townspeople rose up against the establishment there of an Ultra-orthodox centre and in the secular French Hill area of Jerusalem residents demonstrated against municipal approval of plans to build a synagogue and yeshiva complex on the main street of their neighbourhood.

The most striking example of this backlash took place on 11 June when a group calling itself 'People against the Ultra-religious' set fire to parts of a Tel Aviv synagogue, in retaliation against arson attacks on bus shelters by Ultra-orthodox Jews protesting against the posting of advertisements displaying girls in bikinis. President Herzog called it 'a nightmare the devil himself could not have created'. Two days later there were similar attacks on a second synagogue and a religious seminary (*yeshiva*).

Although there are many differences which contribute to the rift between the two cultures in Israel there is none so sharply focused as the confrontation over the Land. This is true because the Zionist movement chose the Land over the Soul, and to secure this preference opted for the use of force rather than negotiation to achieve this goal. The next two chapters discuss how the military came to determine the policies of both the Zionist movement and the state, describe the impact of the military on the psychology of Israelis, then how the Revisionists projected Israel into a fantastic politico-military adventure that brought the country to the brink of civil war.

Notes

1. This description of the 1983 Peace Now demonstration is based partly on an eyewitness account written by Shulamit Hareven, published in *New Outlook*, March/April 1983, and partly on interviews with other participants, including

Avraham Burg, the son of the Interior and Police Minister Yosef Burg. Young Burg was wounded by shrapnel from the grenade that killed Emil Grunsweig.

2. For a detailed analysis of Zionism see *The Zionist Idea: A Historical Analysis and Reader*, by Arthur Hertzberg (New York: Doubleday, 1959). The quotation from Rabbi Kook's writings comes from 'The Land of Israel' on pages 419-20, in the readings.

3. Amos Elon's article appeared in *Ha'aretz*, 1 June 1983.

4. Professor Simon was writing in *The Jerusalem Post Magazine*, 12 March 1982.

5. Ahad HaAm is discussed by Hertzberg in his Introduction, from page 55. Ahad HaAm's statements about the behaviour of the colonists come from an article by Hans Kohn, 'Zionism and the Jewish National Idea' in *The Menorah Journal*, Autumn-Winter 1958.

6. Dr Epstein is quoted by Aharon Cohen in *Israel and the Arab World* (New York: Funk & Wagnalls, 1970), page 67.

7. For a description of Herzl's conversion to Zionism see Desmond Stewart's biography, *Herzl* (London: Hamish Hamilton, 1974), from page 159. The Basle Congress is described on pages 254-5.

8. For a detailed description of the settlers' lives and politics see Amos Elon, *The Israelis: Founders and Sons* (London: Sphere, 1972), Chapter 6, pages 111-53. The quotation is on page 151.

9. See Yosef Goell, 'Anatomy of the Status Quo' in *The Jerusalem Post International Edition*. 25-31 December 1983.

10. See David Landau, *The Jerusalem Post International Edition*, 12-18 August 1984.

11. Yoram Peri in *Davar*, 3 August 1984.

12. Benvenisti's assessment of the two cultures appeared in *The International Herald Tribune*, 21 September 1984.

13. According to a 1986 poll 25 per cent of the secular population view the Orthodox as 'opportunists, liars and charlatans', another 22 per cent associate them with religious extremism and coercion and 13 per cent merely comment on their clothing. See *The Jerusalem Post International Edition*, 16-22 February 1986 and 23 February-1 March 1986.

14. Herzog's address is quoted from *The Jerusalem Post International Edition*, 8-14 May 1983.

15. The Likud leadership's descent to verbal violence has been sharply criticized in the Israeli press by such influential figures as Amnon Rubinstein, former Dean of the Tel Aviv University Law School and Knesset Member for the Shinui Party (Minister of Communications in the 1984 National Unity Government). In an article in *Ha'aretz* on 19 March 1982 he wrote that it was 'becoming hard to distinguish between the lunatic fringe and the mainstream of political life'. Journalists who have energetically attacked the trend include Zvi Barel in *Ha'aretz* (29 December 1983), Shlomo Nahdimon in *Yedioth Ahronoth* (7 August 1983), Amos Oz in *Davar* (November-December 1982), Yoram Sabo in *Koteret Rashit* (27 July 1983) and Dalya Shohori in *Al Hamishmar* (25 January 1982). These are only a few.

2. The Military Preference

We Fight Therefore We Are

Once the Zionists had decided to go beyond the philanthropists' small-scale, haphazard projects for settlement of Jews in Palestine and establish a state there, they had no alternative but militarization. As Menachem Begin wrote in his memoir of the pre-state struggle, *The Revolt*, 'We fight, therefore we are.' Pioneering settlement on the land was in itself offensive paramilitary activity as its object was the seizure of the land from its inhabitants, who had lived on it for generations. From the inception of the Zionist movement the struggle *in* Palestine between newcomers and natives became a struggle *for* Palestine, a war for total possession — of the land, the country, its endowment of geopolitical identity, for a place to live, for human rights and national self-determination.

Theodore Herzl understood this from the beginning of his mission to make political Zionism the ideology of his people and to induce the European powers to secure Palestine for them. He would have preferred that the Jews conquer the Land for themselves but they had no military option. Thus Herzl went round Europe's capitals offering imperialist statesmen Jewish financial support, propaganda promotion and settlers as loyal subjects and, even, secret agents. He was fond of saying 'Qui veut la fin, veut les moyens'. ('He who desires the end, desires the means'.) But while pursuing his external involvements Herzl also generated within the Zionist movement an atmosphere of militancy: he spoke of 'fighting' the scourge of anti-semitism, of 'conquering' the Land, 'capturing' the Diaspora Jewish communities, 'combating' assimilation; the alliances he sought with the rich and powerful were both political and military; he advocated a 'campaign' of deception to get the stubborn Jewish masses to emigrate.

Although Herzl stated in *Der Judenstaat* that the Palestinians would have the same rights as the Jews and described in his novel *Altneuland* a utopian Palestine where natives and newcomers would live side by side in prosperity and harmony, in his private *Diaries* (only published 26 years after *Der Judenstaat*) he described what he really intended to happen.[1] Herzl foresaw a gradual takeover of the country, through land purchase, the exclusion of Palestinian labour from Jewish-owned land, and a boycott of non-Jewish goods. The final stage would involve working the landless and impoverished population across the frontier 'unbemerkt' (surreptitiously). In anticipation of violent opposition to this programme, Herzl proposed the creation of a paramilitary organization well before resistance should manifest itself. Indeed all Jewish youth was to be mobilized and assigned to labour or military battalions for the struggle. In 1901 Herzl—who was clear-eyed and hard-headed about what would have to be done before the state was established—presented a draft charter for a 'Jewish-Ottoman Colonization Association for the Settlement of Palestine and Syria' to the Ottoman rulers, in which he proposed, in Article III, that the Zionists should be given the right to deport the Palestinian population.

The flood of Jewish workers brought by the second *aliya* after 1906 enabled the Zionists to begin the exclusion of Arab labour; in 1907 the first kibbutz was founded as the instrument by which the Zionists sought to secure the land through Jewish labour; also about this time David Ben Gurion and his political comrade Yitzak Ben Zvi (who became Israel's second President) organized a secret defence organization. According to Amos Elon, Ben Zvi's description of the first meeting in his humble room furnished by crates, mats spread on the floor, was

> full of forebodings of things to come . . . one feeling seized all those present . . . they gathered up courage [and they knew] that not by word of mouth shall the nation be saved, nor shall a country be rebuilt by speeches. 'In blood and fire Judea fell, in blood and fire it shall rise again.'[2]

This advocacy of 'blood and fire' was nothing new. On the dark side of even Ahad HaAm's spiritual Zionism were writers who believed that the Jews must revolt against their tradition of political quietism, that the Jewish people could only be reborn by taking up 'the sword' and putting aside 'the Book'. Micah Berdichevski and the poet Saul Tchernickovski were the foremost exponents of the Jewish people's martial renaissance. Berdichevski spoke of 'the blade' as 'the materialization of life' in contrast to 'the Book', which he considered 'the shade of life, life in its senescence'; he demanded that his people 'cease to be Jews by virtue of an abstract Judaism and become Jews in our own right, as a living and developing nationality'. He despaired that the blade and the bow had been discredited in the Bible: 'They shall beat their swords into plowshares.' Tchernickovski desired that the blade and the bow should be used once again in coordination with the plowshare: 'We shall put forth our hands in urging labour, the work that is holy, while grasping the sword. Raise the banners of Zion, O Warriors of Judah.' Tchernikovski in particular had great influence among the youth in the Yishuv and his poetry helped to create the martial spirit necessary to fulfil the task of Zionism.[3]

The first military force, drawing on the left-wing Marxist Poale Zion Party of Ben Gurion and Ben Zvi, was a society of professional watchmen (Hashomer) assigned to Jewish settlements for protection against violent opposition arising out of the exclusion of Palestinian tenants and labourers from Jewish-obtained land. The militant romantic nationalists who joined the Hashomer envisaged the creation of a new, 'tough Jew' who would carry on a 'heroic' struggle through settlement, agricultural labour and physical defence of Jewish interests. Although the Hashomer never had a large membership, it formed a military nucleus which drew up a proposal for the protection of the Yishuv which was adopted by the larger defence forces formed subsequently. Two of the key points in this proposal, mentioned by military historian Amos Perlmutter, were that the force would 'not limit its role to physical protection' but extend it to 'inculcate into' the settlers 'the consciousness that they must defend themselves' and the force must 'serve as the professional-*conspiratorial* armed force of the Yishuv [my italics]'. [4]

There were other attempts, during the First World War, to form the nucleus of a professional army by creating a Jewish legion to serve with the Allies. Eventually a Palestinian-conscripted transport unit, the Zion Mule Corps, and two legions, with Jewish volunteers from the US, Britain and Palestine, were constituted. At the end of the war, demobilized men from these units went into service alongside the Hashomer. In mid-1920 the Zionist Labour parties established ideologically-motivated Labour Legions which practised self-defence along with offensive pioneering, expanding the area of Jewish-held land by establishing kibbutzim on new sites (creating the precedent for establishing paramilitary agricultural settlements, *nahal*, in frontier areas).

The advantage provided to the Yishuv by these forces was offset by the fact that they were supported by partisan political factions seeking to dominate the Yishuv by military force. This bitter factionalism, particularly among the left-wing parties, was somewhat alleviated by the establishment in 1919 of the United Labour Party and in 1920 by the Federation of Trades Unions, the Histadrut. Then in mid-1921 a unified underground organization, the Haganah, was formed under Eliahu Golomb. The new pioneer immigrants from the kibbutzim moved into its ranks as well as the cadres of other community structures. These were the nation-builders who, in spite of ideological competition, mobilized the Yishuv to accomplish the task of capturing Palestine.

In 1929, due to religious conflict in Jerusalem and the upsurge of Jewish immigration, Palestinian militants attacked Jewish settlers in Hebron and Safad and institutions and businesses in Jeruṣalem and Tel Aviv. Even the mild and moderate Chaim Arlosoroff realized that there was 'no way to fulfill Zionism without a transition period in which the Jewish minority takes control of Palestine *as an organized revolutionary élite* [my italics] [4] However, faction-fighting between extreme left and moderate socialists in Palestine and uneasiness in the Diaspora about building up a socialist-dominated army delayed the further development of the Haganah until 1935-6. By then Britain had learnt that the Palestinian Arabs would never acquiesce in the creation of the Jewish National Home and proposed the partition of the country into three areas, a Jewish state (comprising about 20 per cent of the area of the mandate), an Arab state and an area remaining under British control. In spite of vigorous opposition from the Revisionsts, the Zionist Congress accepted the plan, for it gave them a recognized piece of territory. Ben Gurion saw the plan as an opportunity to gain independence: arguing for acceptance he emphasized the immediate need for a state. He saw that the Yishuv was not yet ready to seize control and that it still required British protection, that Palestinian nationalism was growing and that there was an urgent need for a haven for the threatened Jews of Europe.

Ben Gurion, Chaim Weizmann (the President of the World Zionist Organization) and the majority of the Yishuv's leaders supported a policy of restraint towards Britain but the Revisionists, particularly the members of their Betar youth movement, broke with the majority and a group, under Avraham Stern, seceded from the Haganah to form the National Military Organization (the Irgun Zvai Leumi, later splitting to form the Stern Gang faction). The original aim of the NMO was to organize massive illegal immigration, which had been restricted by the British; this was expanded to total resistance to the partition plan and British rule. After robbing a Haganah arms dump the Stern Gang launched a series of terrorist attacks on British soldiers. In spite of the disruptive activities of the Stern Gang, the Yishuv's more cooperative leaders were authorized, after the Arab General Strike began in April 1936, to organize a local police force, the Notrim (Guards). By October, when the violent General Strike ended, there were 3,000 British-armed Notrim in the settlements. Then, although the British authorities proposed that the Yishuv should disband the illegal Haganah in exchange for retention of the legal Notrim, the Government never pressed for the implementation of this proposal and both the Haganah and the Notrim continued to function. Moreover, the revisionist and socialist enemies, Jabotinsky and Ben Gurion, joined forces to persuade the 1936 Zionist Congress to allocate funds for the purchase of arms and to inaugurate a large-scale military training programme for the youth of the Yishuv. The Haganah was reorganized under the auspices of the Histadrut and its headquarters became an embryo ministry of defence.

In 1937, the Notrim, renamed the 'Jewish Settlement Force', was strengthened and permitted to operate outside the settlements, in hot pursuit of armed Palestinian bands. In 1938, the number of special constables was doubled and, early in the year, a flamboyant British officer, Captain Orde Wingate, took to the field with small units of Jewish troops in raids against Arab villages and strongpoints. These units became the 'Special Night Squads' which operated through 1939 in conjunction with the British against Palestinian resistance to the Jewish National Home, and partition.[5] In June 1938 Wingate opened a formal training course for the Squads, proclaiming in Hebrew: 'We are establishing here the foundation of the army of Zion . . . [If your people] fights it will achieve its independence in its own land.'[6] Wingate's biographer Leonard Mosely wrote that Wingate 'was convinced . . that he was engaged in a divinely appointed task, charged like Gideon before him to "go in this thy might, and thou shalt save Israel"'.[7] He achieved a 'magnetic hold' over both the Yishuv and his men, communicating to them his own belief that he, and they, were engaged in a divine mission. He also taught them that they could turn any military situation to their favour with a decisive stroke—a poor practical but good spiritual (morale) doctrine, if one takes into consideration Napoleon's dictum that in war the spiritual is to the material as three to one.

Two of Wingate's most famous pupils were Moshe Dayan and Yigal Allon, and, in Dayan's opinion, 'every leader of the Israeli Army . . . is a disciple of Wingate. He gave us our technique, he was the inspiration of our tactics, he was our dynamic.'[8] But during the Second World War, Wingate, the rebel and hero, was so fixated on his own private war across the Chindwin River in Burma, a diversionary front, that he lost sight of the real campaign in the East. And like Wingate, the Israeli generals long ago lost sight of the magnitude of their military confrontation with the Arabs by focusing on high morale and winning battles rather than following up their series of victories with peace talks.

At the beginning of 1939, the Yishuv had enough men under arms and enough weapons, including an armaments factory manufacturing explosives, mortars and grenades, that Ben Gurion estimated there was sufficient 'to protect settlements against isolated attacks' but 'far from enough for the defense of the Yishuv in case of a general outbreak' of hostilities. From that time on the Yishuv began to build its offensive capacity without which it could never hope to carve out its independent Jewish state.

Because the Haganah as a whole was once again beset by internal wrangling among socialist factions, in 1941 the force's commander, Golomb, created the Palmach, the Haganah's first full-time professional military unit, recruited from the leftist kibbutzim. Trained in guerrilla warfare, the Palmach was the embodiment of Wingate's ideas; its members formed the core of the professional army after the creation of the state; it was the intellectual and operational training ground for the élite of the army. Its officers included Dayan and Allon, Yitzak Rabin, Chaim Bar-Lev, Israel Galili (later a close adviser to Golda Meir). The Palmach's 1,300 original recruits were all Palestine-born, followers of 'Pioneer Zionism', 'new men' who had been nurtured on the redemptive soil of the ancient homeland of the Jews. Ideological soldiers trained in the Palmach were meant to move into the general staff of the Haganah, into industry and politics, carriers of Socialist-Zionism. In training, toughness and discipline the Palmach excelled, but its style was informal and its members were encouraged to exercise personal initiative. Palmach troops gained valuable experience fighting alongside the British in the North African campaigns of World War Two.

At the end of the war, in 1945, the Haganah also had the professional services of the 25,000 demobilized men from the Jewish Brigade which had fought with the Allies in the Mediterranean. In April 1946 the Anglo-American Committee of Inquiry estimated the Haganah's strength at 40,000, to which was added 16,000 Jewish Settlement Police and a war mobilization of 6,000 Palmach; the Irgun Zvai Leumi had 3-5,000 fighters and the Stern Gang 2-300; and senior schoolchildren, of 17-18, were required to do a year's service in communal settlements, as ready replacements for the mobilized fighters.[9]

In November 1947, US Army Intelligence reported to the CIA on 'the consequences of the Partition of Palestine'. According to Stephen Green, one of the first scholars to study the American archives under the Freedom of Information Act, [10] the report said that the Yishuv could muster 200,000 men and women 'who have had some combat and supply experience' and were well-equipped with *modern* weapons. The total troop strength of the Palestinians and Arab irregulars was 33,000, most of whom were poorly equipped and serving in 'quasi-military' organizations — traditional village defence forces. The maximum force the irregulars and the Arab states' armies could field was estimated at 1–200,000. Therefore, it was known *at the time* the partition plan was being considered by the United Nations that the Haganah was capable of implementing the plan and securing the Jewish state.

The Jewish Agency was also confident of military success, but in the spring of 1948 the powers which had backed the partition plan in November 1947 began to retreat from their commitment in the face of overwhelming Arab hostility. Once again following a well-established policy of creating *faits accomplis*, the Zionists put forward by five weeks the war they had planned to start on 15 May. In the first week of April the Haganah mobilized, concluded cooperation agreements with the Irgun and Stern Gang and took delivery of two large arms shipments from Czechoslovakia so that by the 8th the high command was ready to launch the first stage of offensives in operational Plan D (for the Hebrew letter 'Dalet') which was designed to destroy Palestinian Arab resistance through the capture and clearing of their towns and villages. [11] In addition the Haganah had two political objectives: to fuse the area designated for the Jewish state to Jewish settlements *outside* this area and to effect a 'solution' to the problems of mixed population and land ownership posed by the partition plan.

In spite of assurances by the founder of the Haganah that the force did not seek 'to dominate others' it was conceived to 'defend the right of the Jews to come to their country, to settle it and to lead it in a free and sovereign existence'. There was no doubt that the Zionists then, as now, considered the whole of Palestine as 'their country': a Jewish Agency representative confirmed that Ben Gurion, the Agency's head, considered all of Palestine their objective in an interview with an American journalist on 13 May. In a recent interview past President Yitzak Navon said that Ben Gurion was 'always aware of the demographic problem' and Ben Gurion's newly published war diaries show that he wanted the Palestinians to flee the country. [12] By 15 May the Haganah had already accomplished the first stage of its task: secured a corridor (through Arab territory) to Jerusalem (which the Zionists intended to capture although it was meant to be placed under international trusteeship), captured the coast in northern Galilee (which had been awarded to the Arab state) and cleared the bulk of the Palestinian population from Jaffa and Haifa and other areas, producing some 250,000 refugees who were a burden and a hindrance to both their countrymen and the Arab governments. Ben Gurion was in Haifa at the end of April when the city was emptied by the Haganah of its population. While watching from a balcony the spectacle of panic departure, Ben Gurion saw some soldiers preventing a group of Palestinian civilians from going on their way. 'Why are they delaying them? Let them flee,' he reportedly remarked to an aide. It was clear by 15 May, when the Arab armies joined the hostilities, that the Zionists intended to take more than the 55 per cent of the country allotted to them in the partition plan.

On 13 May, the day *before* the mandate ended, US Secretary of State (former General) George Marshall predicted in his daily report on the situation in Palestine that the Haganah would be victorious. By 18 May, this victory was assured because the troop commitment of the combined Arab forces was only 20,000 men, to bolster the 13,000 *organized* Palestinian guerrillas inside the country, while the Haganah had fielded more than 40,000 professional troops and 50,000 militia, outnumbering the attackers by nearly three to one, the reverse of the ratio usually recommended for attackers versus defenders.

Although five Arab states declared war on Israel on 15 May, they only joined battle over a period of two weeks and in a haphazard fashion. In spite of the fact that the Arab governments should have been prepared to do battle for Palestine, they had neither unified command nor plan of attack. One incident, in particular, demonstrated just how hopeless was their war effort. An Iraqi armoured column *en route* to the war via Amman in Jordan halted outside the Philadelphia Hotel while its officers went in to search for a map of Palestine and Transjordan. The manager took down from the wall in the dining room a large tourist map, rolled it up and presented it to the Iraqis, who progressed across the Jordan River, rolled up the hills from the Dead Sea depression to the coastal plain just outside Tel Aviv, where they fought hard and well, but were forced to retreat because they had no support from the other Arab armies. This was the story of the war. The Israeli forces were able to concentrate on one front at a time, switching their mobile units to another front at will or whenever one was activated. Their five-week offensive before 15 May secured for them the territorial continuity and depth they needed to fight from a fortified centre with the Arabs attacking on the periphery, in an attempt to contain the entity they could not undo. And the Arabs could not manage even this. By March 1949, when the first of the armistice agreements was signed, Israel had occupied more than one-third of the territory of Palestine than was awarded to the Jewish state in the UN partition plan. Thus, through fighting, the Zionists solved some of the geographical problems posed by the UN plan, and through their strategy of capturing and clearing Palestinian towns and villages they solved the demographic problems also embodied in the plan: if the Jewish state had emerged in peaceful circumstances it would have been confined to the areas designated for it and it would have had almost as many Palestinian Arabs as Jews. A newly discovered controversial Israeli intelligence report on the Palestinian exodus establishes that more than 70 per cent of those who fled before June 1948 did so because of Jewish military attacks rather than as a result of orders from the Arab governments, as Israeli propagandists have always alleged. And a 'tone. . .of satisfaction' characterizes the report. [13]

In November 1947, when the UN adopted its plan, there were 1,300,000 Arabs and nearly 700,000 Jews in Palestine, the Zionists owning only 6.6 per cent of the land, amounting to some 25 per cent of the cultivable land in the area allotted to the Jewish state. In November 1948, 160,000 Palestinians remained in the 82 per cent of the country under Israeli control, nearly a million were displaced, the majority living in camps in the neighbouring Arab countries or in the central portion of Palestine and the Gaza strip which were in Arab hands. And even this area would have been seized if the Palmach's Southern Commander Yigal Allon had had his way because the Israeli army was certainly capable of achieving the 'border of Eretz Yisrael' along the Jordan and of driving the Egyptians out of Gaza.

But Ben Gurion restrained the military out of fear that the new state would lose the vital support of the Western powers, particularly Britain, which had retained dominance in Jordan. Such prudence was a continuation of the policy of the *tactical* 'moderates' in the pre-state period, of the Zionist leaders who accepted the partition plans and the restriction of immigration as temporary setbacks in the progress towards Eretz Yisrael. This balancing of the desired against the possible, this weighing of the military against the political possibilities, remained the policy of the state until the heir of the Revisionists, the Likud, led by Menachem Begin, took power in 1977.

We Are Therefore We Fight

For those who knew the facts the outcome of the first Arab-Israeli war was, then, a foregone conclusion. But among Israelis there was absolute secrecy about their order of battle, about engagements and objectives — leading to the evolution of a pseudo-mystical atmosphere about Israel's security apparatus and military intentions which Yoram Peri, the Israeli military sociologist, called a 'sanctification' of security. Most observers, including the first US Ambassador to Israel, James McDonald, believed this secrecy was meant to cover weakness. The opposite was true. The Israelis wished to conceal their military superiority so that they would not be restrained by the international community and prevented from reaching their objectives. This concealment gave rise to the myth that Israel was David fighting an Arab Goliath, which generated a great deal of world sympathy for Israel, whose victory was considered miraculous by both Israelis and outsiders, a sign that the messianic age had come. The first victory and its politico-messianic implications ordained a path of military endeavour for Israel.

At least one prominent American, Secretary of State George Marshall, saw the dangers inherent in this state of affairs, and he did so as early as 13 May 1948, *before* the proclamation of the state: the Jewish state could not in the long run survive as a 'self-sufficient entity' in the face of the Arab world's hostility. 'If [the] Jews follow [the] counsel of their extremists who favor [a] contempuous policy toward [the] Arabs, any Jewish state . . . will be able to survive only with continuous assistance from Abroad.' Recent declassification of Israeli state papers indicates that the 'contemptuous policy' which was followed immediately after the establishment of the state made Israel miss opportunities of making peace with Transjordan and Egypt (in the autumn of 1948) and Syria (in the spring of 1949). According to *The Jerusalem Post*'s Benny Morris the Israeli leadership 'failed to respond adequately to serious peace feelers from these countries'. It did not because it had further territorial ambitions and the military machine to fulfil them. Hans Kohn, an authority of modern nationalism, saw clearly what had happened:

> Military victory created the new state; and, like Sparta or Prussia, on military virtue it remained based. The militarization of life and mind represented not only a break with humanist Zionism, but with the long history of Judaism. The Zeitgeist, or at least the Zeitgeist of twentieth-century Central and Eastern Europe, had won out over Jewish tradition. [14]

Since 1948-9 Israel had conducted a prolonged, sometimes military and sometimes diplomatic campaign in what its leaders refer to as its 'war for survival' against the 'implacable hostility' of the Arab world. But the elevation of 'military virtue' to the supreme position it has held, and still holds, was brought about for reasons other than defence: first, to unify politically and socially disparate groupings and create the psychological bonds of nationhood, and second, to expand the boundaries of the state to encompass those of ancient Eretz Yisrael. Israel's 'war for survival' was then as much an internal campaign against factionalism, an exercise in nation-building, as a struggle against the Arabs. This continuous state of war gave the Israeli military a unique centrality in the structure of the state and the lives of its citizens.

Israel emerged after its 'War of Independence' with one, and only one, national structure, the Haganah, renamed the Israel Defence Force (hereinafter the IDF). The only other major structure, the trade union federation, the Histadrut, was a creature of socialism, and mistrusted by the non-Labour portion of the population. Ben Gurion, Israel's first Prime Minister, naturally, saw the IDF as the key state institution, the embodiment of the spirit of pioneering, the instrument to create the 'new Jew' and realize the messianic dream of re-establishing Eretz Yisrael. Such 'militarization of life and mind' was supposed to signify a break with the Jewish past and tradition. Because there was no clear majority party in Israel's political life, Ben Gurion also saw that his moderate Labour Party, Mapai, could use the IDF to achieve political predominance in the new state.

Among Ben Gurion's first acts as Premier were the dissolution of the Irgun and Stern Gang and the disbanding of the élite Palmach units, the absorption of their men by the IDF and the dismissal of their officers. The Palmach had become a powerful, exclusive, left-socialist faction which threatened Mapai's control over the military. Also the distribution of the highly motivated Palmach men throughout the IDF, improved the larger force. The emergence of the state and the legalization of its armed forces did not have the effect of changing, to any great extent, the conspiratorial cast of mind of its command. Indeed it remained as conspiratorial as if it had stayed underground. This was because the task of Zionism was unfinished, and the Zionists knew that if they expected to retain Western financial and diplomatic support, they would have to continue to dissimulate, organize underground, and wait for the opportunity to make their move.

During the 1950s, as before, the Zionists operated on two tracks, assuring the outside world that they were content with the borders achieved by the fighting and defined by the 1949 armistice agreements, while at the same time, declaring in their *Government Yearbook* (1952) that the 'State . . . has been established in *only* a portion of the Land of Israel [my italics]', demonstrating clear dissatisfaction over the status quo. But the new state was too weak economically, too easily pressurized by the Western powers to take further military action at that time.

On one track were the diplomats promoting conciliation and peace with their Arab neighbours while on the second track were the warriors, energetically building up the IDF and the security services. By 1954-5 Israel had two separate political leaderships competing over the implementation of hard- and soft-line policies. But this struggle was really only over means because both the hard- and soft-liners were determined to fulfil the Zionist programme of the Jewish state in all of Eretz Yisrael and were equally hard-headed about keeping everything they had gained on the field of battle. For example, in 1949, the 'hard' Premier David Ben Gurion and the 'soft' Foreign Minister Moshe Sharett held the identical view that the absence of the Palestinians from their homes and lands would enable millions of Jews to settle in Palestine. When the UN put pressure on the Provisional Government to give the Palestinians priority for resettlement, the reaction was described by the UN Mediator Count Folke Bernadotte in these words: 'the Provisional Government would in no circumstances permit the return [of Palestinians] who had fled or been driven from their homes during the war.' Furthermore, during talks with the 'soft' Sharett, Bernadotte learnt 'that when it came to the final shaping of the future of Palestine, the Provisional Government by no means intended to content itself with what had been awarded to the Jews under the United Nations resolution'.[15]

Thus, it was Ben Gurion, with Sharett's help, who put into practice Jabotinsky's doctrine that Israel would have to live behind an 'Iron Wall' which the hostile Arabs could not scale or breach. And he had the personal political reasons mentioned above as well as reasons of state for turning Israel into a fortress state. Ben Gurion, and those round him, sincerely believed that Israel had only to unsheathe its sword and fight and all its problems would be resolved. He insisted that 'the Israel Defense Forces were not a continuation of the Haganah but a renewed manifestation of the Hebrew sovereign force from the time of the Kings of Judah and Israel'. Compromise with the Arabs was unnecessary because Israel would impose a belligerent peace by force of arms. But to ensure that this approach would predominate, the Ben Gurionists had to bring the military into partnership with the political establishment. Ben Gurion did this by removing security from the political arena, making it an autonomous closed area; placing it directly under his control; and maintaining a certain level of tension along Israel's frontiers to achieve for 'security' what Yoram Peri in his study of the Israeli military in politics, *Between Battles and Ballots*,[16] calls 'centrality' in the life of the state.

Ben Gurion set out to make himself the personification of this partnership by taking over the Defence Ministry and habitually wearing battledress. But he did not permit the military to dominate him: he removed or sidelined officers who declined to follow his lead. Neither of the Prime Ministers who followed him, Moshe Sharett or Levi Eshkol, managed to fill his boots, though Eshkol emulated Ben Gurion by keeping the defence portfolio for himself and donned khaki and a black beret when visiting the front during the 1967 war. Under Sharett and Eshkol the IDF simply did whatever it pleased, following a carefully plotted policy of forceful aggrandizement without consulting the Cabinet or Knesset. Such behaviour seriously hampered the functioning of Israel's democratic system.

Ben Gurion succeeded where the others failed because he was the architect of the arrangement: he had held the two posts of Director of the Political Office of the Jewish Agency (succeeding Arlosoroff after his assassination in 1933) and chief of the Haganah (succeeding Golomb on his death in 1945) in the pre-state administration and had laid the foundation for the politico-military partnership then. After the establishment of the state he should have separated the roles of the two groups and promoted cooperative autonomy. But he did the opposite: thus no clear guidelines evolved to determine the military–civil relationship and no mechanism of military accountability was established. This was to have grave consequences in June 1982 when Israel invaded Lebanon.

From 1950 to 1955 Israel's southern and eastern frontiers were zones of confrontation. In international forums Israel was depicted as a small country under threat from its Arab neighbours who sent squads of murderers and marauders across the frontier to kill and maim innocent civilians. But in the Middle East, on the ground, the situation was not as it was portrayed. On the Arab side were Palestinians infiltrating either to return to their homes or to wreak vengeance on their persecutors. They were being restrained by the regular forces of the Arab countries into which they had been expelled. On the Israeli side were young men engaged in a low-to-medium-level war of attrition, the major national objectives of which were to unify the Israeli people by inducing an external threat, to keep the Army up to the mark and sustain a sufficient pioneering spirit among the young to propel them into the frontier areas.

This protracted warfare deeply disturbed Sharett who served as Foreign Minister then Premier during this period and drove him to seek solace in his diary.[17] There he described events in detail, particularly the 'security crisis' along the frontiers which, he said, was based on a 'long chain of false incidents and hostilities we have invented . . . many clashes we have provoked . . . and . . . violations of the law by our men'. This security crisis brought about his downfall and the triumph of the Ben Gurionists who gave the IDF free rein while resisting US and UN efforts to enforce adequate security arrangements. The IDF had to be stretched and hammered, its tensile strength increased for the major military action the Ben Gurionists put on its agenda as early as October 1953—the conquest of Gaza and Sinai, as a first step towards the realization of Zionist ideology, an ideology which, Yoram Peri insists, has as one of its major components military self-reliance or, in the phrase of Max Nordau, a follower of Herzl, 'muscular Judaism'. Thus security was raised to the level of ideology and sanctified, the Army made a 'symbol of identification and glorification, a supreme value', in Peri's words.

But this was not accomplished without controversy, even without setbacks. In October 1953, Ben Gurion, under attack from the 'moderate' faction of Mapai, was compelled to take a vacation from the posts of Premier and Defence Minister and withdraw to a kibbutz in the Negev. His long-time rival Sharett became Prime Minister. By that time he had come to believe that he could negotiate with the Arabs on peace by renouncing Israel's claims to additional territory, offering compensation to the displaced Palestinians and abandoning the policy of 'retaliation', as Israel called its forward military policy. But Ben Gurion had no intention of letting go of power: before leaving he appointed hard-line colleagues Pinhas Lavon to the Defence Ministry, Moshe Dayan as Chief of Staff and Shimon Peres as Director-General of the Ministry. Ben Gurion left behind a time-bomb with a short fuse. Sharett became Acting Premier on 14 October; on that very night between two and three hundred Israeli troops crossed into the demilitarized zone on the Jordanian frontier and attacked the village of Qibya with automatic weapons and mortars, then dynamited 41 houses and a school, killing 69 civilians.[18] The unit to carry out this action was a new formation, based, as the Palmach had been, on Wingate's 'Night Squads'; it was 'Unit 101' commanded by Major Ariel Sharon. But this force, unlike the Palmach, which had had both ideological motivation and social purpose, had no reason for existence other than conducting provocative raids to maintain tension along the frontier. After its blooding at Qibya, Unit 101 was the only formation in the IDF to carry out such night attacks and demolition raids. Dayan later evaluated its importance by saying that 'it operated with such brilliance that its achievements set an example to all other formations in the army'.

Sharett condemned the raid (which he had tried to stop) in the Cabinet, raged in his diary and tried to justify it to official Americans who paid a protest call. In the communiqué on the raid Ben Gurion (who attended Cabinet meetings still) insisted that the Army must be excluded from responsibility and civilians living in the border area blamed for having taken, in Sharett's words, 'justice into their hands' (exactly the phrase West Bank settlers would use thirty years later to justify acts of violence against Palestinian civilians). Sharett, under protest, agreed because the Army, as Israel's national institution, had to remain unstained and irreproachable.

On 19 October, Ben Gurion again dominated the Cabinet session, speaking for 'two and a half hours on the army's preparations for the second round [of the "War of Independence"] . . . [He] presented detailed figures on the growth of the military force of the Arab countries which [he said] will reach its peak in 1956.' Which meant that Israel would have to go to war before then. On 23 October a group of American Zionist leaders was told by General Mattityahu Peled that (according to Sharett 'the Army considers the present border with Jordan unacceptable' and 'is planning war in order to occupy the rest of Western Eretz Yisrael,' i.e. to the Jordan River (presumably leaving Eastern Eretz Yisrael, that is the Balfour Declaration promises in Transjordan, for a later date). And on 31 January 1954, Sharett wrote that Dayan had presented to the Cabinet 'one plan after the other for "direct action"' designed to produce 'war with Egypt'.

But, because the Cabinet reacted unfavourably, Dayan was diverted by Ben Gurion to plans for military action against Syria with the aim of occupying southern Syria while the weak Damascus Government was occupied with putting down a revolt of troops in Aleppo. In February 1954, Ben Gurion and *his* Defence Minister Lavon presented a plan for the creation of a Maronite Christian state in Lebanon which would enable Israel to seize the southern, predominantly Shiah Muslim portion of the country which, in Ben Gurion's opinion, would 'be of no use to [the Maronites] and . . . not constitute a disturbing factor'. In March an Israeli bus was attacked between Eilat and Beersheba and ten passengers killed, allegedly by infiltrators from Jordan. Ben Gurion's immediate reaction was that Israel should 'occupy Jordanian territory'. However, after taking the testimony of the four survivors of the bus attack, the American chairman of the mixed Jordanian-Israeli Armistice Commission officially stated that it was 'not proved that all the murderers were Arabs' and in a confidential report to the head of the entire truce supervisory operation stated that the attack was designed to heighten tension along the frontier and create problems for the Sharett government, intimating that, as Dayan himself admitted to journalists at the time, the gang could have been 'local'. The climate of uncertainty over the identity of the attackers enabled Sharett to prevent the sort of retaliation Ben Gurion and the military had in mind, but only for a short time. On the pretext of another, minor incident, on 28 March, the Army launched a Qibya-type operation against the village of Nahlin, near Bethlehem. Discussing the incident with his senior aide Teddy Kollek, now Mayor of Jerusalem, Sharett asked whether Israel was heading for war or wanted to prevent it. Kollek replied that 'the army leadership [was] imbued with war appetites [and] completely blind to economic problems and the complexities of international relations'.

The Nahlin incident increased Arab vigilance against infiltrations from their side of the border so the Israelis had to resort to penetration raids by small parties from Unit 101 to maintain and heighten tension. On 14 April Sharett wrote in his diary that the US State Department was convinced of the existence of 'An Israeli plan of retaliations' which was designed 'to bring about a war'. The Israeli military was also poised to sabotage Egypt's relations with the West. In July 1954, during the crucial phase of the negotiations betweeen Egypt and Britain over the evacuation of the Suez Canal Zone, the Israelis activated a group of saboteurs in Egypt which bombed the British and American cultural centres, British-owned cinemas and several Egyptian post offices and public buildings in Cairo and Alexandria. The Egyptian Jews among the saboteurs were caught and eventually tried and convicted. Two were hanged and the others given long terms of imprisonment; three of the Israeli commando officers escaped and the fourth committed suicide. This became the celebrated 'Lavon Affair' which thereafter tainted Ben Gurion's participation in politics, and strengthened Sharett's hand in the Cabinet.

In spite of Egyptian anger over the Lavon Affair, Sharett initiated a series of contacts with the Egyptian President Gamal Abdel Nasser through various UN, US and British mediators. The most notable effort was that of the British Member of Parliament Maurice Orbach who travelled back and forth between Cairo and Tel Aviv. Although the proposal put forward by Sharett was limited to specific steps for the reduction of tension, Orbach indicated in an article he wrote for *New Outlook* in January 1965 that there had also been exchanges of a more general nature which had produced a draft peace treaty between Egypt and Israel. While these contacts were going on Sharett prepared the way in the Knesset to obtain a formal mandate to negotiate peace, which he did in September. He was able to do this because the military activists had been discredited by the Lavon Affair. Concerned that a commission of inquiry might delve too deeply into the Lavon Affair and further discredit the military, Dayan attempted to organize a coup against Sharett and was supported by this by Ben Gurion. But the more level-headed, younger elements of Mapai refused to go along with the plot. [19]

From Militarization to Militarism

The Americans stepped up efforts to bring the two sides together and, as an inducement to negotiate, offered the Israelis a security pact. But at the same time the Egyptians, still smarting from the humiliation of the Lavon Affair, launched a series of small-scale raids into Israel, including an infiltration near Rehovot, 30 kilometres from the Gaza border. On 17 February 1955, Ben Gurion returned to the Ministry of Defence and ten days later attended the Cabinet meeting 'carrying rolled-up maps'. The IDF responded with a massive operation against an Egyptian military base in Gaza on 28 February, which left 38 Egyptian soldiers dead and 30 wounded. Less than a month later, Ben Gurion proposed the permanent occupation of Gaza and was turned down by the Cabinet. The security pact with the US was also rejected, on the insistence of Ben Gurion's supporters, meaning the military establishment, because as Dayan complained, 'it would put handcuffs on our military freedom of action'.

This rejection was a turning point for Israel. It demonstrated that the country had tipped from *militarization* to *militarism*. It was a qualitative change affecting the society's spiritual and material welfare. If Israel's militarization had been purely defensive the Government should have welcomed a pact which would have guaranteed the country's security from external attack. But the military establishment would be neither contained nor restrained. In May, Dayan explained the refusal to Israel's ambassadors in Western capitals:

We do not need . . . a security pact with the US: such a pact will only constitute an obstacle for us. We face no danger at all of an Arab advantage of force for the next 8-10 years . . . thanks to our infinitely greater capacity of assimilate new armaments.

Israel was militarily unassailable but it still required freedom of action. Dayan said:

Reprisal actions which we couldn't carry out if we were tied to a security pact are our vital lymph . . . they make it possible for us to maintain a high level of tension among our population and in the army. Without these actions we would have ceased to be a combative people and without the discipline of a combative people we are lost.

In his study entitled *Military Organization and Society*,[20] Stanislav Andreski defines four different types of militarism: idolization of the military, the peacetime militarization of the society, rule by the military, and the galvanization and preparation of the society for war. In Israel all of these varieties of militarism had assumed control. Dayan himself personified the military idea of the 'new, heroic Jew' of the poet Tchernikovski: Dayan was born on a kibbutz, the forcing house of Zionist militancy, a disciple of the flamboyant Wingate, a loner and 'Arab fighter', a man who profoundly believed that his people's problems could be solved by the use of force. Both the Ben Gurionists and the military establishment agreed that military ideals and sentiment must prevail in Israeli society and set about inculcating them. By joining in partnership with the politicians the military establishment assumed partial responsibility for ruling Israel; and the military partner did not have to answer to the electorate. Israel did not become a military dictatorship, but a militarized democracy, its democratic processes somewhat curtailed by the politico-military partnership.

Furthermore Israel's powerful military class, even caste, regarded military efficiency, *per se*, as the paramount interest of the State, and sought to achieve and sustain such efficiency through near continuous warfare. As Sharett commented in his diary entry for 26 May 1955, when he was given a report of Dayan's meeting with the ambassadors,

. . . the question of peace is non existent . . . [Israel] must calculate its steps narrow-mindedly and live on its sword. It must see the sword as the main, if not the only instrument with which to keep its morale high and to retain its moral tension. Toward this end it may, no — it must — invent dangers . . . above all let us hope for a new war . . . so that we may finally get rid of our troubles and acquire our space.

On the day after the Gaza raid Ben Gurion launched a personal campaign against Nasser, the Arab leader he considered Israel's most dangerous enemy, perhaps because Egypt had shown readiness to negotiate with Sharett, even after Ben Gurion had returned to the Cabinet, even *after* the Gaza raid. Nasser adopted the strategy which Israel had used so effectively over the years: on the diplomatic level he pressed the US to step up its mediation efforts and when it demured, initiated a new mediation approach through the American

Quaker Elmore Jackson;[21] and, on the military level Nasser demanded that the US supply his army with defensive weapons. Washington refused, so by the end of summer Cairo signed an arms deal with Czechoslovakia (the Middle East's second Czech deal, the first having been concluded by Israel in 1947-8).

The Third Jewish Kingdom

On 1 October Sharett recorded in his diary the text of a classified cable from Washington in which Israel's 'partner' (named in the diary as Kermit Roosevelt of the CIA[22]) discussed the confusion and anger the Czech arms deal had caused there and commented on Israel's surprising 'silence'. 'When our man asked . . . whether we are expected to go to war, the answer was: "If, when the Soviet arms arrive, you will hit Egypt — no one will protest."' In the Cabinet meeting on 3 October, both Ben Gurion and Isser Harel, chief of counter-espionage (Shin Beth), concluded that the message was a green light for Israel to mount an operation to topple Nasser and destroy his army, lift the blockade of the Tiran Strait, force the relocation of Palestinian camps away from Israel's frontiers and secure additional territory. In November Ben Gurion resumed the premiership, relegating Sharett, once again, to the Foreign Ministry, which Ben Gurion demoted to the status of an information agency charged with explaining rather than making policy. The 'security crisis' enabled Ben Gurion and the militarists to take complete control. From February the US Joint Chiefs of Staff *repeatedly* predicted a lone victory over the Arabs for the Israelis. From March Israel began to receive shipments of modern arms, including advanced Mystère Mark II fighter planes from France, as well as British Meteor night-fighter jets and the latest tanks; from August through October Israel plotted with France and, finally, secured Britain as a third partner.

Then, on 29 October 1956, the US Joint Chiefs of Staff issued a special intelligence report which stated that the Israeli mobilization was sufficient to occupy some Syrian territory, penetrate Egypt to the Suez Canal and hold portions of Sinai, open the Tiran Strait and attain dominance over all the frontline Arab airforces. On that very day Israel entered the war and, as in 1948, it entered the field on a footing of overwhelming superiority: 45,000 Israeli troops, supported by 155 warplanes, faced 30,000 Egyptians with 70 operational combat planes. But Israel was not content with its individual superiority: it was assisted by some 70,000 British and French troops, supported by 240 combat aircraft, 130 warships of which 7 were aircraft carriers, 80 transport ships, etc.[23] This time the simple ratio of attackers to defenders was nearly four to one, well over the recommended three-to-one ratio.

On the bank of the Suez Canal Ben Gurion jubilantly proclaimed the 'Third Jewish Kingdom'. But Moshe Dayan, his Chief of Staff, was apprehensive about 'our capacity to hold our own in the political campaign which now begins'.[24] And he was right. Israel had made two major political miscalculations: it had brought in the old regional imperialists, Britain and France, and the attack had been timed for the eve of the American Presidential election because Israeli strategists believed that the US Administration would be both inattentive and powerless to act. But the Russians had also chosen that time to intervene in the Hungarian insurrection, making it impossible for the US to condemn one intervention and condone the other. The US cut aid on 31 October and refused to reopen the pipeline until Israel committed itself to withdrawal, which was done by Knesset vote on 14 November.

On that day a disappointed Dayan told the world press that Israel could have won the war on its own in seven days — which it may have indeed done. But there was a risk that the fighting might have dragged on and, though American intelligence reports estimated that Israel could sustain a state of war for 90 days, three times longer than it was projected the Arabs could do, a protracted conflict would have had severe economic consequences for Israel. There was another, more important reason that Israel chose to act in concert with Britain and France: in spite of its militaristic spirit, its high level of combat training and offensive posture, the Army command could not justify heavy casualties to the people of Israel from whom the troops were drawn. Israelis liked, and still like, fighting, but not dying. The military establishment has been, and still is, bound by an iron law of low casualties, and must devise its wars with this law firmly in mind — which explains why Israel took on partners in 1956, why it waited until 1967 to fight the war it was strong enough to fight in 1956, why it was shaken by the concerted Arab attack in 1973, and why it had to fight again in 1982 in order to dismiss the failure of 1973 from the public mind.

Dayan tried to delay the pull-back as long as possible, telling his officers at each stage to 'smile' and 'not make it a tragedy'. Nevertheless Ben Gurion had to face down a near-mutiny of angry officers who were determined to keep the spoils of their war. After the completion of the Israeli withdrawal, in the spring of 1957, Dayan went abroad on extended leave and early in 1958 resigned as Chief of Staff to begin a political career. The 1956 failure demonstrated clearly how Israel's dependence on external aid dictated its politico-military policy. A quarter of a century later, Menachem Begin, then Prime Minister, in an oral message to the Lebanese Maronite Phalangist militia leader, Bechir Gemayel, disappointed over Israel's refusal to intervene on his force's behalf against Syria, defined Israel's attituded about gains and losses: 'I said that the State of Israel in her wars, which are not over yet, knew how to lose territories and regain them and much more. One needs patience and the right perspective.' [25]

The Preventive War Strategy

The Ben Gurion perspective prompted Israel to give priority to military development between 1957 and 1963, by purchasing armaments from abroad and enlarging and diversifying its own defence industry (under the tutelage of Shimon Peres, first Director-General of the Defence Ministry, then Deputy Minister). Then in June 1963 the grumbling repercussions of the Lavon Affair forced Ben Gurion to resign for the last time, hoping, still, to be better able to influence policy from outside the Cabinet than in. Another 'soft' politician in the Sharett mould, Levi Eshkol formed a government and once again a struggle for power ensued between the Ben Gurionists (including Dayan and Peres) and the Mapai majority led by Eshkol. In September, Peres, in a Knesset speech, demanded that Israel continue to pursue a policy of military expansion enabling the IDF to launch 'preventive' wars whenever the Israeli military establishment estimated that an Arab country, or any combination of Israel's neighbours, should threaten Israeli predominance. This was an advancement of the 1950s 'method of provcation-and-revenge' designed to produce wars so Israel could obtain its territorial objectives.

In the contemporaneous estimation of the Israeli journalist Simha Flapan,[26] the adoption of the preventive war concept would lead to 'the domination of military over political considerations and the overwhelming predominance of offensive weapons in the military sphere'. In combination with the older practice such a concept promoted the utilization of local clashes 'to increase tension' in order to create 'opportunities to deliver a "crushing blow"' as well as acquire additional territory. Flapan painted a bleak picture of the situation: 'Armaments have become a substitute for foreign policy and instead of being a means of defense have become an end in themselves to which all other aspects — economic, political and international — must be subservient.'

But, since the tip-over from militarization to militarism had occurred in 1955, when Israel refused to conclude the security pact with the US, Flapan's warnings came at least eight years too late. The process of transformation had long been completed. The adoption of the 'preventive war' strategy was not a sign of incipient militarism but of advanced militarism; it brought about the realignment within the Israeli politico-military establishment which precipitated two wars, 1967 and 1982, and facilitated the rise of the Revisionist militarists after 1977.

Prelude to the 1967 War

Levi Eshkol's prime ministership almost exactly paralleled that of Moshe Sharett a decade earlier, demonstrating that the partnership between the politicians and the military was an uneasy one. The push-me-pull-you nature of this relationship imposed a pattern on Israel's war-making, the politicians holding back and the military propelling the country into war.

As soon as the Eshkol government took power the military began to act independently of the Cabinet Defence Committee, focusing its 'provocation and revenge' policy on Syria this time. The IDF occupied the demilitarized zones along the Syrian frontier and, though the Israelis had just completed a project to pump water from Lake Tiberias to the Negev, the IDF prevented the Syrians from preparing a much less ambitious diversion scheme well within

Syrian territory by shelling the project site. Then on 1 January 1965, the movement for the National Liberation of Palestine, Al Fatah, launched an unsuccessful operation across the Lebanese border into northern Israel: the militarists in Israel had the pretext they wanted for raising the level of violence. The first operation was followed by other pinprick commando raids across the Lebanese frontier, and later the Jordanian and Syrian frontiers as well. The targets of these raids were houses, water installations and roads. In spite of the fact that the governments of all three Arab countries tried to prevent these infiltrations, the cycle of raid and counter-raid resumed.

Mapai was already split between the Ben Gurionists and the pro-Eshkol faction over Ben Gurion's belated and unjust criticism of the failure of the generals (specifically Yadin and Allon) to conquer all of Eretz Yisrael in 1948-9 (a purely cynical about-face of the man who stopped them from doing so). If Dayan had been in charge, Ben Gurion claimed, the 'map of Israel would have been different', that is to say complete. Once again the Lavon Affair was resurrected. The Executive Committee of Mapai split, 40 per cent for Ben Gurion (including backing from the Army high command) 60 per cent for Eshkol (with the support of the Histadrut, retired Army officers, civil servants, industrial managers and the intelligentsia). Ben Gurion lost the struggle for dominance in Mapai and left the Party taking Shimon Peres and Dayan with him to form Rafi, a move which severely diminished Ben Gurion's influence as Rafi never elected more than ten members to the Knesset.

During the Mapai crisis there was the sensational spy trial and public hanging of Eliahu Cohen, an Egyptian Jew who had been operating so successfully in Damascus that he had penetrated the Government. The Cohen affair had the same impact on Syria as the Lavon Affair had had on Egypt: in 1966 Syria changed its policy from curbing to encouraging Al Fatah. In July and August clashes between Israel and Syria became full-scale battles. At the very time Eshkol and his Foreign Minister Abba Eban were trying to promote a new peace initiative and requesting that the US conclude a security pact with Israel, the military stepped up pressure on the Cabinet to authorize the IDF to deliver its 'crushing blow' to Israel's enemies. Chief of Staff Yitzak Rabin warned Syria that Israel's 'reprisal raids' would be directed against the regime. This led Damascus and Cairo to conclude a mutual defence treaty on 4 November. Three more Fatah raids, undertaken from Jordanian territory, prompted a massive Israeli attack on the Jordanian village of Samu. This operation was conducted in daylight by a large force of Regular Army units supported by aircraft. The tactics of Wingate and Sharon had come out into the open: the man responsible for this escalation was Ezer Weizman, the airforce chief. Weizman, like the Herut leader Menachem Begin, believed that all of Eretz Yisrael belonged to the Jews and he was prepared to act on this belief. And there were many other Israelis who agreed with him in senior army and intelligence positions.

In January 1967 a series of clashes occurred between Israel and Syria in the Golan Heights and each side accused the other of a troop concentration on the border. On 13 May the Egyptians were informed of an Israeli build-up along the Syrian frontier; the information was said to have come from the Russians and to be false although there is evidence from a still-suppressed UN observer report that the Israelis had in fact mobilized in strength and concentrated troops along the frontier. On 16 May the Egyptians asked for withdrawal of the United Nations buffer force that had been stationed along the 164-mile frontier since 1957 and announced their intention of occupying Sharm Al Shaikh in Sinai, overlooking the Strait of Tiran from where they could close the Gulf of Aqaba to Israeli shipping, the opening of which had been Israel's sole gain from the 1956 war. This move gave the Israeli military the pretext it was waiting for, but it never constituted the serious threat it was claimed to be. The Israeli Chief of Staff, Yitzak Rabin, said in an interview with *Le Monde* in February 1968, 'We knew that Nasser did not intend to attack.' And this was confirmed by Premier Menachem Begin in a speech to the Israeli National Defence College on 8 August 1982.

Completing the Land of Israel

Having reached the brink of war, the Eshkol Cabinet held back, creating a ten-day government crisis which was only resolved on 1 June by the establishment of Israel's first national unity government, and, on the insistence of the Army (threatening a coup) the appointment of Dayan as Defence Minister or, as the military preferred, 'Minister of War'. From the moment of Dayan's appointment, the war for 'Greater Israel' was ensured. According to Dayan's biographer, Shabtai Teveth, 'Dayan's desire' for this end 'coloured every aspect of his political thinking and expression'. [27] On 4 June the new government decided to go to war the following morning, rubber-stamping the decision taken by the IDF months before. This time Israel would go it alone, with the covert approval of the Johnson administration in Washington and the support of four US reconaissance aircraft with American crews flown in from Moron, a NATO base in Spain, to a base in the Negev. [28]

These planes were meant to assess Israel's capability to win the war in the space of a week. According to Stephen Green, the Americans believed that the Israelis would capture territory during this war which could be used as a bargaining counter with the Arabs to achieve a peace settlement. It was clear that the Johnson administration either did not know, or refused to acknowledge, why the war was being fought. The Israeli military establishment had finally manoeuvred the Arabs into giving them a *casus belli* on the basis of which they could secure the 'space' they coveted. According to Sharett, Ben Gurion himself said that it would be worthwhile paying an Arab a million pounds to start a war in order to have just such an opportunity. In the event, Israel had to make a much more substantial investment in time and money to achieve what it wanted, the capture of the remainder of Western Palestine, considered the heartland of Eretz Yisrael, and the securing of the Golan Heights. The victorious Dayan became the 'King of the Territories'.

Within days of the ceasefire the Israeli Government called for direct negotiations with the Arabs, promising an exchange of 'territory for peace'. It looked as if Israel might, at last, manage to negotiate an end to the 20-year state of war with its neighbours. However Israel also adopted two unpropitious policies. First, nearly a quarter of a million Palestinians who had either fled across the Jordan River during the fighting or been expelled by the Israelis afterwards were not permitted to return to the West Bank or Gaza. Second, the Eshkol government's policy over withdrawal was in fact an acceptance of principle rather than a commitment to pull back from virually *all* the areas occupied during the war. The Government insisted instead that Israel should have 'security borders' and 'strategic depth', binding itself to the military's interpretation of how withdrawal should be conducted.

In mid-July the Cabinet unofficially adopted a plan submitted by then Brigadier Yigal Allon under which Israel would retain control of unpopulated areas of the West Bank, amounting to about 30 per cent of its area, certain sectors of Sinai, and all of Gaza and the Golan. The idea behind the Allon Plan was that Israel would retain access to the territories without incorporating their population. By September, the US, which had regarded Israel's victory as an 'opportunity' to bring about regional peace negotiations, began to realize that 'Israeli objectives may be shifting from [its] original position [of] seeking peace with no . . . territorial gains toward one of expansionism.' What was clear was that the US had gained a mistaken impression of Israel's 'original position' from the politicians in Eshkol's broken-backed government; the military establishment had undertaken no commitment to hand back the territory achieved in the fighting and had no intention of doing so. It would have been surprising if it had been otherwise because the fathers of the state, men like Ben Gurion and Dayan, were fully committed to the extension of Israeli rule over the entire Land, for which they had been fighting since the 1930s. After the 1967 war — when Israel was divided on the issue of the territories — Ben Gurion reflected the thinking of the military when he said that he wanted both peace and territory.[29]

Former Chief of Israeli Military Intelligence, Governor of the West Bank and UN Ambassador, now President Chaim Herzog affirmed in his book *The Arab-Israeli Wars*[30] that the military establishment really believed that Israel could have both territory and peace: Israel's overwhelming victory had so traumatized the Arab world that 'an atmosphere' had been created,

> . . . particularly in Israel, indicating that an end had been reached in the wars of Israel with various Arab countries . . . From a military point of view, Israel was now in a much stronger position than it had ever been . . . this fact enhanced the prospects for peace negotiations. This time Israel would be negotiating from strength.

And this was a strength which, indeed, it has possessed since its establishment without entering into negotiations involving give and take.

The Iron Wall

The Israeli military expected, and demanded, Arab capitulation. But this expectation showed that both the military and the militarists in Israel had totally failed to understand the Arab character. Three weeks after the ceasefire, the War of Attrition began along the Suez Canal, a war which went on until August 1970. Then on 1 September, at Khartoum, the Arab states proclaimed that they would not recognize, negotiate with or make peace with Israel. The War of Attrition took two forms: Egyptian artillery barrages across the Suez Canal and Palestinian commando raids across the other frontiers. In response the IDF, at first, adopted a policy of massive retaliation against the commandos, which resulted in an unexpected military reverse for the IDF: the rout of an armoured unit, supported by paratroops, at the Jordanian town of Karameh in March 1968. Then in October 1973 the Egyptians, Syrians and Iraqis launched a surprise war against Israel, a war which cost the Iraqis their airforce, the Egyptians the eastern bank of the Suez Canal, Syria more territory in the Golan Heights — and the Israeli military its self-esteem, and its self-confidence.

In 1973 the Arabs caught the Israeli military napping. Once the war was brought to a conclusion with Israel shocked but not defeated, the military attempted to reform itself. A new government under former Chief of Staff Rabin was installed, Israel's first premier from the military establishment. In 1978 the IDF sought once again to demonstrate its massive superiority by launching the Litani Operation against PLO commando bases in southern Lebanon. Designed as an action to neutralize and disperse the Palestinians, it did neither and cost Israel many casualties. After the withdrawal of its army from Lebanon, Israel became dependent for the security of northern Israel on a local Lebanese force, under Major Saad Haddad, which it had created in 1976 to man a buffer zone along the frontier. Israel was learning that political, and even military, problems could not always be solved by the application of force.

Transformation of the IDF by the Occupation

Because Israel did not opt for peace through the return of the occupied territories to the Arabs, the IDF assumed the task of ruling those areas and was rapidly expanded to fulfil that role. Israel had reached another turning-point: it had become a military empire. Between 1967 and 1973 military costs trebled, rising to nearly six times the 1966 expenditure in 1975, then slipping back to about four times that sum in 1983.

The victory of 1967 reinforced the 'centrality' of security in Israeli life, improved the position of the military élite *vis-à-vis* the politicians, and conferred on the IDF control of the occupied territories, which comprised some 70,000 square kilometres—compared with the 26,000 square kilometres within the 1949 boundaries. IDF rule was extended over nearly a million Palestinians as well as the Syrian Druse population which had remained in the Golan Heights. The IDF assumed civil, administrative and security functions in the territories, making it the sole political agent in those areas — and giving it an expanded, additional political role in internal Israeli politics. As an ideological army bound to the major tenets of Zionism, the IDF could not but devise a policy, contrary to international law, of changing the status quo in the occupied territories in order to secure them for Israel. The policy it devised involved acquisition by settlement; it was embodied in the Allon Plan which envisaged military settlements in 'security zones', as a first-stage absorption programme.

The Political Consequences of the Victory

The popular reaction in Israel to the 1967 victory strengthened the hand of the military: it recreated the euphoria of 1948-9 which had sprung from the belief that Israel's emergence had been a miraculous event and that the new state would be sustained by other such miracles. The economic boom that followed the 1967 war added to this conviction that Israel was about to fulfil its God-given promise. In the aftermath of the 1967 victory, the men and women who had been disappointed over the territorial 'compromise' of 1948-9 banded together to form the 'Land of Israel Movement'. Its manifesto, of August 1967, stated, in part: '. . . The whole of Eretz Yisrael is now in the hands of the Jewish people . . . we are bound to be loyal to the entirety of our country . . . and no government in Israel is entitled to give up this entirety.' Among its influential signatories were: Israel's first Nobel Prize winner, the poet S. Y. Agnon; the widow and brother of its second President, Yitzak Ben Zvi; Isser Harel, the first head of Shin Bet (counter-espionage); the son of the Revisionist leader Vladimir Jabotinsky; Dr Israel Eldad, a member of the Stern Gang leadership who became the ideologue of the radical Gush Emunim settlers group and a founder of the militant Tehiya Party; Knesset members from Mapai, Herut and the National Religious Party; distinguished poets and novelists; seven high-ranking Army officers; and the organizers of the World War Two Warsaw Ghetto Rising. Most of the signatories were born before 1920, many within five years on either side of the turn of the century. They were representative of Israel's original Zionism and formed a powerful lobby in combination with Israel's younger, Palestine-born military élite.

Within three months of the occupation, the real positions of the 'Greater Israel' lobby and the Government were as follows: the lobby would give 'not one inch' while the still dominant soft-liners in the Cabinet would cede 70 per cent of the West Bank, most of Sinai and nothing else. (The present position of the latter is that 60 per cent of the West Bank and a portion of the Golan *may* be negotiable, as all but a few thousand square metres of Sinai proved to be.) Because on the eve of the war Mapai had been too indecisive to rule its coalition partners and had been obliged to form a national unity government, the Mapai core was even more subject to pressures from a wider range of parties than before.

From 1967 until 1977, when the Revisionist Likud formed its first government, the concessionist position of the soft-liners was steadily eroded. The militants demanded full implementation of traditional Zionist ideology through the extension of Israeli sovereignty over the territories. But the process of erosion did not go unchecked in the diplomatic sphere. In May 1970, under strong US pressure, Israel was compelled to accept the provisions of United Nations Security Council Resolution 242 calling for Israeli withdrawal from virtually *all* Arab territory occupied in 1967. The price of this capitulation was the resignation from the Cabinet of Menachem Begin's Gahal Bloc (which preceded the Likud formation). At the same time the Government also capitulated to internal pressure to follow up the occupation with the settlement of the territories. In order to accomplish this, the Government resorted to an elaborate deception: 'settlers' in military uniforms were assigned to zones specified in the Allon Plan as being required for 'security arrangements'. By 1973, 44 military 'settlements' had been planted in these zones while civilian settlement took place at Kiryat Arba in upper Hebron (to recreate a Jewish presence in that 'historic' Jewish town) and in East (Arab) Jerusalem which had been annexed in 1967 and its municipal boundaries expanded to include Arab suburbs where land was expropriated for 'urban development'.

The politician who made the crucial contribution of the disguised annexation strategy — beyond the Allon Plan — was, understandably, the military leader who secured the new territories, Moshe Dayan. In 1973, before the October war, he put forward a comprehensive set of proposals, later incorporated into a Cabinet document by Israel Galili, Prime Minister Golda Meir's personal adviser. These proposals provided for the settlement and complete integration — by fostering economic dependence and building integrated road, electricity, water and communications networks. Dayan's objective was to prevent the 'repartition' of the Land of Israel, without formally annexing the territories and giving status to their Palestinian inhabitants. He believed that the 1967 war had imposed a test on the Israelis: 'If we believe [in it] and want it, the map of Israel can be determined by ourselves. [But only] if we are prepared for the political and military struggle and if we are prepared to carry the full burden of the struggle.' [31] Dayan was well aware that the line he proposed meant an endless war with the Arabs, but that was a price he was prepared to pay.

The 1973 war brought down Dayan as Defence Minister because he was held responsible for the failure of Israeli intelligence to foresee the Arab attack and for the slow response of the IDF. The IDF idol was cracked; its policy of hegemony in the security sector questioned. But the politico-security crisis generated by the war made Dayan's plan for the territories all the more acceptable to the politicians; the ruling Labour Alignment increased its insistence on the need for 'strategic depth' while Herut and the religious parties considered Israel's victory in adverse circumstances as proof positive of its ability to hold and defend the borders of Eretz Yisrael.

Militarization of the Society

Since independence, most Israelis have measured the effectiveness of their state in terms of its military power — ostensibly because of the 'Arab threat', but really because the task of Zionism, the securing of the entire Land, had not been completed at independence. The early Zionists had elevated the Land to a position of sanctity, and the Yishuv subsequently raised the State to a position of equality with that of the Land. And the State was moulded by David Ben Gurion whose view of its nature and its relationship with its citizens had come out of his Eastern European Marxist experience: according to Aharon Bechar, one of Israel's foremost political writers, 'For Ben Gurion, the state was above all, as if the state was not supposed to serve its citizens, but on the contrary, the citizens were supposed to serve the state.' [32] As their primary service to the state was military, the IDF was placed alongside the Land and State on the altar of Zionism. And the society was 'militarized'.

General Yigal Yadin summed up the situation: 'The Israeli citizen is a soldier on eleven months annual leave.' The average Israeli male must serve for 36 years, first for three years as a conscript, then in the reserves for between 45 and 70 days a year. A man's status in the society is determined by his service record, which must be produced when he applies for higher education, work or securing government-provided financial assistance.

Secondary-schoolchildren join the paramilitary Gadna ('Regiments of Youth'), or the Herut-sponsored Betar movement which has its own military-type units. There is also 'volunteering' in schools and neighbourhoods for civil defence and other security-orientated work. Like the youth of Sparta, adolescent Israelis are regimented then vigorously trained to a peak of physical fitness, resembling, as Amos Elon admits, the German youth of the 1930s. Their model is the kibbutznik, who has been raised from birth in a patterned community, who represents, Elon asserts, 'manly vigor' in contrast to the 'weakness of exile'; kibbutzniks are 'redeemed' by their close connection with the land (though kibbutzim had become increasingly less agricultural and more industrial); they are pledged to élite units in the Army and to professional military service. [33] Accounting for only 4 per cent of the population, kibbutzniks hold nearly a sixth of parliamentary seats, farm one-third of agricultural land, and contribute a quarter of the Army officers — a quarter of the casualties in the 1967 war were kibbutzniks.

Personality cults have grown up round particular military figures, with Moshe Dayan being the most admired high-ranking officer. As Ben Gurion put his stamp on the State, Dayan impressed his own on the IDF. He was the officer most responsible for the informal style of the military. In 1938, while training non-commissioned officers of the Jewish Settlement Police, Dayan wrote a manual of field training, later adopted by the Haganah. Dayan objected to British Army insistence on kit and drill and fixed formations. He devised guidelines for a more flexible guerrilla-type force which emphasized results rather than forms. The formation of mobile field companies and Wingate's 'Night Squads' gave Dayan wide scope for promoting his methods.

And he was encouraged by the likeminded guerrilla commander Yitzak Sadeh who told his men to break the rules, be 'irresponsible', if a task demanded it. Flexibility to an 'irresponsible' degree became the code of the Haganah, then the Palmach and the IDF. This independence of action became maverick-ism when the military establishment, or certain portions of it, or the Defence Minister, took upon themselves the responsibility of launching military initiatives with wide-ranging political repercussions. The most striking example of such behaviour is Defence Minister Dayan's ordering the head of Northern Command, on 9 June 1967, to attack the Syrian Golan Heights — without the knowledge of the Chief of Staff or the approval of either the Prime Minister or the Cabinet. Or, as it later became clear, the acquiescence of the US Government. But then Dayan would brook no interference in achieving his territorial ambitions.

If Dayan was the IDF's pragmatic maverick, its spiritual maverick was, and still is, Meir Har-Zion, described by Amos Elon as 'the living symbol of a "new", cold blooded Jew with an armour plated conscience'.[34] Born a third generation Sabra in 1934, of Orthdox Russian stock, Har-Zion spent his adolescence on a kibbutz from where he set out on exploratory adventures, sometimes with his younger sister, into the border regions and Arab territory. Such behaviour, courting danger and flouting authority, was a craze among the generation which grew up just after the founding of the state. Har-Zion joined the Army in 1953, becoming a paratroop commando in Ariel Sharon's Unit 101, the élite unit of the most élite corps. Har-Zion became a brutal legend, 'an Israeli version of the Indian Fighters in the American Wild West', said Elon, 'killing Arab soldiers, peasants, and townspeople in a kind of fury without hatred . . . twice or three times a week for months' until he was critically wounded in a raid on a Jordanian police station. While in the Army he continued his lone forays into Arab territory — on one he shot and killed a Jordanian soldier and on another he knifed two bedouin in revenge for the killing of his sister, who had been on one of her private jaunts. For the latter murders he was arrested, then released without trial, at Ben Gurion's behest — setting a precedent which has been followed in cases of other soldiers and civilians who have 'taken *the law* into their own hands'.

The IDF is twice the size it was in 1973 — this growth taking place between 1974 and 1979 — and has eleven divisions in comparison with six in 1973; it costs the country well over a third of its budget. Tel Aviv University's Joffe Centre for Strategic Studies (in *The Middle East Military Balance 1983*) gives the IDF's strength as 170,000, both professionals and conscripts, who number over 100,000, the airforce having the highest percentage of professionals. In addition there are 340,000 trained reservists, of whom 26,700 are on reserve duty at any one time.[35] The Defence Ministry also rules and runs a large military industrial sector, with 25 per cent of all industrial workers engaged in its factories. The arms industry has become the largest single enterprise in the country, accounting for 16 per cent of Israel's total industrial exports: 40 per cent of the output of the military industries being exported, 60 per cent consumed by the IDF (consumption being 500 per cent over the 1967 level). The IDF also operates a radio station and a publishing house which produces both the armed forces magazine and a great volume of pulp novels on the exploits of Israeli soldiers for popular reading.

Professional soldiers are retired early, at 40, so they can make second careers in business and politics. Yoram Peri makes the point that 'Israel is the only Western democracy in which the army is a crucial avenue into top political jobs.'[36] Since its founding Israel has had one prime minister, two deputy prime ministers, two foreign ministers, two defence ministers (or three, if Rabin is counted twice), two agriculture ministers (Dayan and Sharon) and many other key ministers 'who came to their posts directly from the military'[37]. Some officers founded their own political parties: Dayan was one of the three who created Rafi in 1965, Ariel Sharon ran as the candidate of his own 'Peace of Zion' Party in 1977, in that year a group of officers led by Yigal Yadin took 12 Knesset seats for their 'Democratic Movement for Change' Party; in 1984 Ezer Weizman (who had become a Cabinet minister representing the IDF in 1969) and former Chief of Staff Raphael Eitan established their own parties, Yahad and Tsomet, respectively, and former General Mattityahu Peled formed the Progressive List for Peace. Furthermore, almost all the former members of the military establishment who are currently at the centre of the political scene — Shimon Peres, Yitzak Rabin, Ariel Sharon, Ezer Weizman — are Ben Gurionists, men who participated in the military victories of Israel and who helped to build its Iron Wall.

Traffic has not always been from the military to politics: in 1973 a large number of ranking reserve officers returned to service in high-command positions, including Sharon, Chaim Bar-Lev (then Minister of Commerce and Industry) and the former Commander of the Airforce, Mordechai Hod. Conflicts along party lines resulted, particularly on the southern front, and erupted into a 'generals' war' when the Arab–Israeli fighting ended.

Some politicians made their careers in the intelligence establishment, like former Likud Prime Minister Yitzak Shamir and President Chaim Herzog.

Of Israel's 100 retired generals some have moved into the senior jobs in public enterprise — notably the Koor Industries (owned by the Histadrut) which employs 9 per cent of industrial labour, the Electricity Corporation, the Paz Petroleum Company, the Dead Sea Potash Works, the Steel City Works, Israel Oil Refineries — and in the private sector, cement, computers, banking, one of the major supermarket chains. Other generals have become university rectors and professors and mayors. And there are, of course, the thousands of retired officers below the rank of general who return to civilian life while keeping a foot in the Army through their ration of reserve duty. Thus, in Israel a unique situation emerged in which the military was politicized through its partnership with the political establishment and the political and economic spheres were militarized through their penetration by retired officers.

The movement out of the security-defence establishment into the political establishment, the bureaucracy, the industrial sector brought about the creation of what Yoram Peri calls an upper social class, whose members enjoyed close intrapersonal relations, thought and behaved alike, displayed similar approaches to political issues, and had many interests in common. They also share a special attitude toward the country's security problems, formed during their membership in pre-State underground military organizations or during IDF service.

And the one thing they all agreed upon was the dictum, quoted by Peri, that 'foreign policy should serve defense policy'. [38]

All these factors have produced an entrenched military establishment which will not retreat from its political role, seriously reduce its expenditure (after the 'drastic' 1984-5 cuts the military still consumes 40 per cent of the state budget) or reform its ranks. In May 1986 the extent of the military's influence in the society was revealed when a report prepared by the former Chief of the Planning Department of the General Staff broke through the military censors into the media. In the document, prepared for the General Staff by a military academic, Dr Emmanuel Wald [39] bluntly catalogued the weaknesses of the IDF which, according to Wald, has deteriorated from war to war, beginning with 1967. Wald was particularly critical of the upper echelon of the General Staff which, he said, was 'mediocre' and promoted increasingly mediocre officers, and of these officers putting their own self-interest and job security ahead of the operational capability of the IDF. He criticized the IDF's order of battle, its lack of tactical ability (demonstrated in Lebanon), its over-reliance on tanks since 1967 and its dependence on massive logistical arrangements. The report had been ignored by both the Defence Minister and the Chief of Staff then suppressed by the IDF high command which sought only to preserve its image rather than reform. This unwillingness to accept criticism and to make necessary changes propels the IDF into military actions — like the Litani Operation and the Lebanon war — because of its need to prove itself after poor performances. Hence the 1982 war was designed to wipe out the humiliation of the Arab surprise attack of 1973 and the next war will have as its motive the re-establishment of the IDF after its humiliating withdrawal from Lebanon.

The debilitated IDF that Ariel Sharon took over in 1981 was unable to resist the force of his will to launch the messianic 'War for Greater Israel' and propel the country into the uncertain era of the messianic militarists.

Notes

1. Herzl's real intentions are revealed in *The Complete Diaries of Theodore Herzl*, five volumes, edited by Raphael Patai and translated by Harry Zohn (New York: Herzl Press and Thomas Yoseloff, 1960). The reference: Volume I, pages 38 and 51.

2. Amos Elon in *The Israelis: Founders and Sons* (London: Sphere, 1972), page 124.

3. Hertzberg, *The Zionist Idea*, pages 294-5. And, Leonard Victor Snowman, *Tchernichowski and his Poetry* (London: Hasefer Agency for Literature, 1919), page 26.

4. Amos Perlmutter, *Military and Politics in Israel: Nation Building and Role Expansion* (London: Frank Cass, 1969), page 5. For the quotation from Arlosoroff's *Jerusalem Diary* see ibid. page 13.

5. Britain's contribution to the Zionist war effort is described in two articles by David Ben Gurion in *The Jewish Observer and Middle East Review* of 20 and 27 September 1963.

6. An account of Wingate's assistance is given in the second. Wingate's career was a spectacular failure because of his love of waging private wars.

7. This is shown clearly in *Gideon Goes to War*, by Leonard Mosely (London: Arthur Barker, 1955).

8. Ibid., pages 55-64, quoting Dayan.

9. The *Report 1946* of the Commission (Cmd 6808) issued by His Majesty's Stationery Office.

10. Stephen Green's *Taking Sides: America's Secret Relations with Militant Israel* (London: Faber, 1984), based on new material obtained under the Freedom of Information Act, is a very important contribution to the political history of the Arab-Israeli conflict. For military estimates see pages 68-70. Other material on US policy, including quotations, comes from this work.

11. Plan Dalet is described in detail in *The Edge of the Sword: Israel's War of Independence 1947-49* by Nethanel Lorch (New York: Putnam's, 1961), pages 87 ff.

12. Navon's interview appeared in *The Jerusalem Post International Edition*, 13-19 November 1983. Ben Gurion's war diaries *Yoman Hamilhama Tash "Ah-tash" At* edited by Gershon Rivlin and Elhanah Orren (Tel Aviv: Defence Ministry Press, three volumes, 1983). They were reviewed at length by Benny Morris in *The Jerusalem Post International Edition* , 22-28 April 1983.

13. The 24-page report entitled 'The Arab Exodus from Palestine in the Period 1/12/1947-1/6/1948', dated 30 June 1948 was discussed and analysed by Benny Morris, *The Jerusalem Post*'s diplomatic correspondent, in the first quarterly issue of *Middle Eastern Studies* (London) of 1986. This IDF internal report was discovered by Morris in the papers of a leading Mapam figure, Aharon Cohen, who had been the director of the Party's Arab Department. The fact that the document remained for 37 years among the private papers of a leading leftist politician is a clear indication of the loyalty to the cause and State of Zionists considered to be the most ready to make concessions to the Arabs.

14. Professor Kohn was a 'spiritual' Zionist immigrant to Palestine who left before the emergence of the state. The quotation is from 'Zion and the Jewish National Idea' in *The Menorah Journal*, Autumn-Winter 1958.

15. Sharett was quoted by a shocked Mediator, Count Folke Bernadotte in his memoir *To Jerusalem* (London: Hodder & Stoughton, n.d.), pages 189-90.

16. Yoram Peri, *Between Battles and Ballots: Israeli Military in Politics* (London: Cambridge University Press, 1983), page 19.

17. Moshe Sharett's *Personal Diary* was published in the original Hebrew in 1979 by the *Ma'ariv* press. Extracts have appeared in a number of journals and books. The quotations used come from the writings of Livia Rokach, the daughter of Sharett's Minister of Interior, which were published in *The Journal of Palestine Studies* (Beirut), Number 35, Volume IX, No. 3, Spring 1980, and *Israel's Sacred Terrorism* (Belmont, Mass.: A.A.U.G., 1980). Sharett fixed October 1953 as the earliest date he became aware of Israeli plans at the highest level for the occupation of Sinai. Sharett, about to succeed Ben Gurion as Prime Minister, met with

President Ben Zvi, Ben Gurion's collaborator in the founding of the military arm, who sounded out Sharett on the possibilities of Egypt starting 'an offensive which we could defeat and follow with an invasion' of Sinai.

18. Qibya was discussed in both the Rokach material and Stephen Green's book, in Chapter 4, where Dayan is quoted.

19. Apropos the coup contemplated in 1954, Ehud Ya'ari was quoted in Rokach's book, page 63.

20. Stanislav Andreski, *Military Organization and Society*, second edition (Berkeley, California: University Press, 1968), pages 184-6.

21. Jackson waited for 27 years to publicize the effort, which he did in November 1982 through the press, before writing about it at length in *Middle East Mission: The Story of a Major Bid for Peace in the Time of Nasser and Ben Gurion* (London and New York: Norton, 1983). The title was curious because the person most responsible for scuttling the peace effort was Ben Gurion.

22. Because the reference to Kermit Roosevelt as Israel's 'partner' codenamed 'Ben' will raise eyebrows, the reference is in Rokach's book at the bottom of page 54, and she is quoting Sharett. Isser Harel, the Shin Bet chief, explained Roosevelt's position to the Cabinet: '. . . the U.S. is interested in toppling Nasser's regime . . . but it does not dare at the moment to use the methods it adopted to topple the leftist government of Jacobo Arbenz in Guatemala [1954] and of Mossadegh in Iran [1953] . . . It prefers its work to be done by Israel.' (Sharett's entry of 3 October 1955, page 55.) The ups and downs of Britain's campaign to get the Americans to take on the job of toppling Mossadegh are described by C. M. Woodhouse in his memoir *Something Ventured* (London: Grenada, 1982). Woodhouse's CIA contact was Roosevelt who was known as the key figure in the Shah's return to power.

23. Estimates from Green, Chapter 6.

24. The exchange between Ben Gurion and Dayan was mentioned in Shabtai Teveth's *Moshe Dayan: The Soldier, the Man, the Legend* (London: Quartet, 1972), page 323.

25. Menachem Begin is quoted by Itamar Rabinovich, *The War for Lebanon 1970-1983* (Ithaca and London: Cornell University Press, 1984), page 166.

26. Simha Flapan, the editor of *New Outlook* for many years, was quoted extensively by Stephen Green on page 190 of his book.

27. Dayan's obsession with the achievement of the entire Israel is described by Teveth on page 331.

28. Green supplied the details of the operation involving US reconaissance aircraft from interviews with one of the airmen participating, page 204. For such acts of military collusion there is no freedom of information. Green discusses the naive estimation of Israeli aims on page 199.

29. There has recently been some controversy in Israel over Ben Gurion's position on the occupied territories, with both hawks and doves saying he agreed with them. Although towards the end of his life Ben Gurion undoubtedly did say to journalists that he thought the territories should be exchanged for peace agreements with the Arabs, such a line was inconsistent with his life's work. After all, he was the man most responsible for achieving the wholeness of Eretz Yisrael. At the time Ben Gurion made his 'dovish' statements he was an old man out of power, wondering what history would make of him: he preferred to be regarded as a man of peace rather than a man of war, like Bar Kokhba (whose significance is described in the next chapter). The territory-and-peace position was completely

in character.

30. Chaim Herzog, *The Arab-Israeli Wars* (London: Arms and Armour Press, 1982), page 195.

31. Dayan is quoted by Rael Jean Isaac in *Israel Divided*, page 132.

32. Aharon Bechar's article appeared in *Yedioth Ahronot*, 2 September 1983.

33. Amos Elon, op. cit., page 243.

34. Ibid., pages 241-2.

35. The number of reservists was given in *Ha'aretz*, 14 December 1984.

36. Yoram Peri, *The Military Industrial Complex in Israel*, published by the International Centre for Peace in the Middle East, January 1985, pages 4 and 52.

37. Peri quoted from *The International Herald Tribune*, 20 October 1983.

38. Peri in *The Military Industrial Complex*, pages 52 and 82.

39. In May 1986 Wald's report became a major media event. It was then, after a 'cooling off' period following his forced resignation from the IDF, that Wald broke silence. He aired his views in an interview with Ran Edelist in the May issue of *Monatin* which had attempted to break the story in December 1985 but had been stopped by the censor.

3. The Rise of Messianic Militarism

The Messianic Undercurrent of Zionism

Theodore Herzl's Zionism was purely secular and practical: he would deliver his persecuted people to a safe haven where, in the spirit of his, and our, time they would found a national state. His was a political messianic doctrine but one divorced from the religio-historical variety. Herzl, a modern messiah, was committed to leading his people to any territory where they might establish themselves. For Herzl, and some of his collaborators, Palestine was merely a device for 'capturing the communities', particularly the masses of Eastern Europe. But in the First Zionist Congress in 1857 Herzl was compelled to accept that his movement must focus on Palestine as the 'legend' which would move his people. When Herzl continued to resist the pre-eminence of the Land in subsequent Congresses the majority simply ignored him and concentrated their energies on Palestine. Herzl's élitist messianism was expanded in this way to provide the real motive force of Zionism: a 'return' by Jews to their ancient homeland. This became the principal messianic genus, the belief which united the disparate parties in the movement.

But there was a dark sinister undercurrent which, according to the Israeli novelist Amos Oz, has

> Flowed within Zionism almost from the beginning, the current of nationalistic romanticism and visions of greatness and mythological renewal, the current of longing for kingdom and blowing trumpets and conquering Canaan in a storm, the national superiority complex based on military nostalgia in the guise of gross religious impulses, the conception of Israel as one giant act of revenge for the historical 'humiliation' of the Diaspora.[1]

This undercurrent flowed through all the ideological schools in the movement, each of which brought its own special type of messianism. Among these were the Marxist and socialist messianics who fixed the polity of the state long before its establishment, cultural messianics who made Hebrew once again a living vernacular tongue, spiritual messianics who would raise Israel to a superior moral and ethical plane, physical messianics who would rebuild the Jewish physique debilitated by centuries of exile, and military messianics who would re-establish Israel by the sword. The latter were given a boost by the powerful undercurrent that flowed within the ideology as a whole.

The ideologue of the last group was Vladimir Jabotinsky, a journalist like Herzl but without his Austro-Hungarian refinement. Jabotinsky came to believe in the efficacy of the sword above all other instruments; and he saw that, once founded, the state would be obliged to live by the sword. He formulated a theory which was adopted not only by his ideological heirs, the Revisionist-Herut-Likud, but also by the Labour leadership. Jabotinsky wrote:

> Neither to the Palestinian Arabs nor to the Arabs from other countries will we be able to offer 'compensation' for the loss of the land of Israel . . . Zionism will persist by relying on power, behind an *iron wall* that the native population will not be able to breach.

Ben Gurion also believed that Israel would never be accommodated by the Arabs, and acted on that belief; Dayan predicted that the Jewish state would not gain the 'voluntary' acceptance of the Arabs. For them and their colleagues in the military establishment Israel would have to fight until it pacified the Arabs, or gained hegemony over them. Furthermore, Jabotinsky's map of Eretz Yisrael, drawn to provide room for mass immigration from holocaust-torn Europe, tallied with the map religious messianics were determined to achieve; they were prepared to fight for this vision, then live behind an 'Iron Wall' if that was the price of having Eretz Yisrael. The combination of Jabotinsky's Iron Wall theory with his map and the messianic undercurrent of Zionism produced *messianic militarism*.

Messianic Politics

Although it was firmly committed to the 'completion' of the Land, when this was achieved in 1967 the Labour rulers of Israel could not openly advocate annexation of the territories occupied because their allies, particularly the US, had approved the war on condition that the territories occupied would be exchanged for peace. As a result, Labour was forced to devise a stratagem for maintaining control over the territories, a stratagem which fell short of outright annexation: this stratagem was the Allon Plan mentioned earlier. This Plan placed the territories in the sanctified security realm, making their disposition dependent upon Israel's security requirements — as decided on by Israel alone. The Allon Plan enabled Israel to satisfy its foreign friends by making it appear that the fate of the territories was undecided while at the same time creating a military presence in 'security areas' designated in the Plan.

Labour was compelled to resort to such a devious policy because it was under challenge from the supporters of annexation, especially the Land of Israel Movement, who saw the 1967 victory in messianic terms. The society was torn by a partisan competition involving what Shubert Spero, Professor of Jewish Thought at Bar Ilan University, aptly called 'messianic politics',[2] in which the rightist parties tried to outbid the Government on the issue of the territories. This competition coincided with the increasing disillusionment of the Oriental community with Labour's social and economic policies and the gradual shift of Oriental voters to the Likud — which, in addition to giving them positions in the party hierarchy, promised them consumer goods and provided a demagogic authoritarian style of leadership they found attractive. Thus the voting power of the majority of Orientals was harnessed by the ultra-nationalist and ultra-religious messianics.

The ultra-nationalist messianics are the deepest pessimists of Zionism. They have been described with eloquent clarity by Reuven Alberg, a former teacher of history at the religious Bar Ilan University: they believe that 'Jewish life in the Diaspora is basically impossible, that it will end either in destruction or assimilation.' Thus 'the Jews of the world . . . should be rounded up and forced to settle' in Israel. (And the Palestinians should be 'shipped to Iraq'.)[3] The font of these ideas was a certain Avraham Sharon (formerly Schwadron) who lived in Israel some 25 years ago and his doctrines have been reinjected into contemporary messianic politics by the influential right-wing ideologue and publicist Israel Eldad and Tehiya Party Knesset Member Zvi Shiloah. They would have Israel hold onto the West Bank for messianic reasons — though they also bolster their arguments with the security case.

Israel Eldad, the most intelligent spokesman of this school, also favours the annexation of southern Lebanon to secure the headwaters of the Jordan River (which were included in the Jewish state in a map prepared for the Zionist Organization by an agronomist and submitted to the Versailles Peace Conference in 1919) and the reoccupation of Sinai to regain both space and oil. Eldad joined in the founding of the Tehiya Party to oppose withdrawal from Sinai. He disagrees with the strict constructionists of Herut who insist that Israel should occupy the East Bank of the Jordan River to a point just south of Amman, the capital of the modern state of Jordan (an area also included in the 1919 map). Zvi Shiloah would occupy a large part of Syria, to restore the Israel of King David. Some of these expansionists would give the Palestinian, and other Arab, inhabitants of the territories they would seize, 'autonomy' — control over their religious affairs and daily life — but would grant no rights over the land on which they live (as would Begin); others would buy out the natives and arrange for their transfer (Shiloah); while some would force them to leave (Eldad, a substantial section of Gush Emunim, Kach). They want nothing less than the reinstatement of the Jewish people in the historical Eretz Yisrael as it was at the peak of its power and its greatest territorial extent. Then it could absorb the immigrants they would bring to the country or force to move there.

Such secular imperialists have joined forces with the militants of the religious parties, including from the non-Zionist Agudat Yisrael, to form the vanguard of the second culture, to become what Shlomo Avineri, former Director-General of the Israeli Foreign Ministry, called 'the territorial school of Zionism'.[4] Its followers like to consider themselves as the 'Lovers of Eretz Yisrael', implying that those who disagree with them love the Land less than they do or not at all. Their first success came in 1970 when the first national unity government, then under Golda Meir, permitted a group of settlers organized by Rabbi Moshe Levinger to establish Kiryat Arba as a Jewish suburb of the Arab town of Hebron. The political partnership of Yigal Allon, whose Plan included the area where Kiryat Arba was established, and Menachem Begin, who believes that Jews have the right to settle anywhere in Eretz Yisrael, pressurized an ambivalent Cabinet to permit the settlement, the first to be established by civilians, which *The Jerusalem Post* called, 13 years later, 'nothing but a springboard for the takeover of Hebron by the Jews'.

Pressure for settlement was intensified from the Diaspora as well: the 28th Zionist Congress, which met in 1972, unanimously adopted a resolution affirming the Jewish 'right' to Eretz Yisrael. The 'Complete' Israel activists had their second success in 1975 when Shimon Peres, then Defence Minister, permitted the Gush Emunim movement to establish a civilian settlement at Kaddum in 'Samaria', within the bounds of a military outpost and another for 'security workers' at Ofra. The real settlement push began after the election of Israel's first Revisionist government in May 1977. The coalition that came to power included the Likud (43 seats), Ariel Sharon's 'Peace of Zion' Party (2 seats), the National Religious Party (12 seats), the non-Zionist Agudat Yisrael (4 se、 s) and Moshe Dayan (1 seat), who, without leaving the Labour Party, became Foreign Minister. It is significant that this, the original small coalition was joined by the ultra-religious Agudat Yisrael Party. One of its venerable Knesset Members Menachem Porush explained: 'It [was] the first time I felt I was dealing with a Jewish government.' [5] Agudat Yisrael was particularly attached to Begin because that Party was convinced of his sincerity as a believer and felt that Begin would promote the Jewish character of the state. Agudat Yisrael's agreement with the Likud was both firm and useful as it saved the coalition on many occasions.

The coalition gained another 12 seats in October when Yigal Yadin agreed to become Deputy Prime Minister, giving the Government 77 seats out of the 120 total. Shortly after the election Prime Minister Begin asserted his government's unequivocal position on the occupied territories: 'I believe that Judea and Samaria are an integral part of our sovereignty. It's our land . . . It was liberated during the 6-day war . . . It is our land.' [6] As such, he said, it did not require annexation. And as usual, to buttress his position, he brought in the security argument. Then the 29th Zionist Congress reasserted 'the right of the Jewish people to settle in all parts of the Land of Israel', and, in reaction to the United Nations resolution branding Zionism as a form of racism, offered a new definition of Zionism in line with the drift towards the religio-historical variant: 'Zionism . . . is the uniquely Jewish movement for national liberation and *redemption* based upon our *messianic* dreams and upon practical action for self-realization [my italics].' [7] In the four years between the 29th and 30th Congresses (the latter held in 1982) 205 settlements were established in all areas of Eretz Yisrael: 103 by the Jewish Agency within the Green Line (in Galilee, the Negev, Arava and in northern and central Israel) and 102 by the World Zionist Organization's Settlement Unit in the West Bank, Golan Heights and Gaza. Following Zionism's pioneering tradition, the presence of settlers was meant to stake a claim to the places where they settled.

Messianism and Archaeology

In addition to the methods of settlement and conquest, the Zionists relied on a third, that of archaeological exploration, to lay claim to portions of the Land. The person most responsible for expanding Israel's 'archaeological frontiers' was the soldier-politician Yigal Yadin.[8] The son of a pioneering archaeologist (Eliezer Sukenik, who recognized the authenticity of the Dead Sea Scrolls), and a pioneering educationalist, Yadin became chief of operations of the Haganah in 1947 when he assumed responsibility for drawing up and implementing the plan for the war of Israel's establishment. And in 1949 he became Chief of Staff of the IDF. After resigning in 1952 (in disagreement with Ben Gurion's political appointments in the Army), Yadin gained renown as the excavator of the well-known messianic digs at Masada, the site where Jewish rebels made their last stand against the Roman Legions, and at the 'Bar Kokhba caves', another place connected with Jewish resistance to outside rule. During the first dozen years of exploration Yadin attempted to fix the biblical account of the conquest of the Land to archaeological facts. In 1960 he even mounted a modern military operation to recover Jewish documents in the Jordan valley border area. Then, while investigating some caves at Nahal Hever he discovered the Bar Kokhba letters which captured the imagination of the modern Israelis and made archaeology a national preoccupation.

In 1964 Yadin began his well-publicized dig at Masada, overlooking the Dead Sea, where in AD 73 a band of zealots fought the Romans then committed suicide to prevent being captured. In the estimation of Abraham Rabinovich, Masada was to have 'the most powerful emotional impact on Israel and abroad' of all the 'excavations ever carried out in the country'. Yadin dramatized his find in such a way as to bring events in ancient Israel alive to ordinary people and by so doing added a new dimension to messianic politics. And, he brought the IDF into the field of archaeological exploration, giving the military yet another sphere of influence and endeavour.

In the opinion of Meron Benvenisti the elevation by early Zionists of Masada as a symbol of the modern Jewish state resulted in the creation of a 'secular cult'. Then the myth of Masada was given substance by Yadin's discoveries. And three years later the myth was, according to Benvenisti, 'fused together with 2000 years of Jewish history'[9] when the IDF captured the Old City of Jerusalem wherein lies the site of the Second Jewish Temple which was destroyed in AD 70.

Messianic Risk-Taking

If the mountain fortress of Masada became modern Israel's symbol, the final revolt led by Bar Kokhba in AD 132-5, which ended in another last stand of zealots at the Betar stronghold, was chosen by the Zionists as the example of Jewish resistance to alien rule which must be followed by the new state. The Israeli scholar who has closely analysed the impact of what he calls 'the

Bar Kokhba syndrome' is Yehoshafat Harkabi, Professor of History and International Relations at the Hebrew University of Jerusalem, a former IDF general and Director of Military Intelligence. Harkabi adopts the view of classical Jewish scholars that the Bar Kokhba revolt against Rome was an ill-advised disaster which 'stemmed from a mistaken assessment of the possibility of defeating the Romans'; it led to the dispersion of the Jewish population of Judea and exile. Harkabi asks why modern Israel 'should treat their error as something to be revered; how is it that a people comes to admire its own destruction and to elevate [the revolt] which enabled the Gentiles to subjugate it'.[10] This 'positive evaluation of the revolt' has serious consequences for Israel because its people and its leaders have permitted themselves to believe that Israel can achieve anything it desires if it only dares, causing them to take unacceptable risks in every area of national endeavour.

The election of the second Likud government in July 1981 was itself an example of serious risk-taking. Yosef Goell, *The Jerusalem Post*'s political commentator, summed up the performance of the first Likud government in the following words: 'The Begin government began malfunctioning from Day One in July of 1977.'[11] The Party was divided by internal conflict, it had to resort to election economics (providing a mass of consumer goods to attract voters) and military adventurism (the bombing of the Iraqi nuclear reactor and the PLO headquarters in the Fakhani district of Beirut) to win. And even then the Likud only managed to tie with Labour (each securing 48 seats in the Knesset), after the defection of its right wing to form Tehiya (Guela Cohen and Yuval Ne'eman) and of part of its moderate 'La'am' faction to form Telem with Moshe Dayan. The Likud's coalition partner, the National Religious Party, secured 13 seats but lost four through the secession of the Oriental members to form Tami, the 'Movement for Tradition in Israel', which appealed to the Oriental electorate on the basis of Jewish tradition rather than Orthodoxy, as defined by the Ashkenazi rabbis of the NRP.

The NRP's price for its support was a coalition agreement which included the promise to apply Israeli sovereignty to the occupied territories at the end of the five-year period of autonomy granted to the Palestinians in the 1979 Camp David Accords (after which, according to Egypt and the US the territories would join in some sort of entity with Jordan). Begin formed his second government on the basis of a majority of only 61 seats out of 120. But this did not deter Begin who, in the words of Professor Daniel J. Elazar of Bar Ilan University, '. . . treats a majority of one as if it were a landslide'.[12]

Yitzak Berman, Minister of Energy in this and the 1977 government, described the shift that occurred with the introduction of the second Likud Cabinet: 'The premise on which the new policy was based was that Israel could simply ignore the reactions of the outside world, with the exception of the United States, which should be treated with more caution' but could be expected to support Israel because of its own strategic interests.[13] Begin's choice of close confederates confirmed this shift towards isolationism and adventurism. The two most important of these confederates had opposed the peace Begin himself had concluded with Egypt. They were Foreign Minister

Yitzak Shamir and Defence Minister Ariel Sharon, whose devotion to the completion of Israel certainly equalled that of Begin. The former Cabinet had included three political chameleons, Moshe Dayan, Yigal Yadin and Ezer Weizman, who left because he disagreed with Begin's interpretation of the Egypt-Israel agreements. Both Begin and Sharon followed an autocratic style in dealing with the Cabinet: they took decisions and merely applied for approval.

The Messianic Militarists

Menachem Begin became a militant Jewish nationalist in the Polish Betar movement (named after the Bar Kokhba site), becoming its head before the Second World War. In 1938 Begin joined a group of young Betar activists to urge the leadership of the secessionist National Military Organization (Irgun Zvai Leumi) to begin a campaign of armed resistance against Britain in Palestine, anticipating Jabotinsky's decision to do so by a year. Once in Palestine Begin led the 'Revolt' designed to drive Britain from the country. Begin came to speak only of 'Jews', not 'Hebrews' or 'Israelis' and to consider Israel the domain of the entire Jewish people. His life was devoted to the establishment of the Jewish state; his rhetoric was dominated by the Holocaust; he referred often to God in his political speeches. Like Herzl, who wanted to lead his people to safety, Begin had a messianic vision of himself. He wanted to be remembered 'as the man who set the borders of the Land of Israel for all eternity'. [14] To do this he had to launch a war: first, against the Palestinians in the territories who resisted the occupation and demanded self-determination; and, second, against the Palestine Liberation Organization which was gaining influence on the international scene. Begin's pre-state military organization, the Irgun, and his political party, Herut, had always been marginal in Israel's wars: the Revisionists had neither won battles nor taken territory. The ascendancy of Jabotinsky's Iron Wall doctrine meant little to Begin, because he had not accomplished it. The Litani Operation of 1978, conducted under the first Begin government, had been a limited action which had not secured the objective of expelling the PLO fighters from southern Lebanon. And Begin was smarting under the 'humiliation', as Benny Morris put it, [15] of being forced to sign a ceasefire with the PLO after the 1981 'mini-war' of attrition across the frontier. Begin had to reclaim his, and Israel's, honour by proclaiming what Professor Yehoshafat Harkabi called an 'Etzel War' ('Etzel' being the Hebrew acronym for 'Irgun Zvai Leumi'), a war which was 'an incarnation of the ideas of Etzel' designed to 'produce big results, big slogans'.

The man Begin chose to conduct this war, Ariel Sharon, had been refused the Defence Ministry in Begin's first Cabinet. On one occasion Begin reportedly said he would not put Sharon in that position because he feared a 'putsch', but the Prime Minister's reservations were also due to the fact that Sharon was not a disciple of Jabotinsky, never a member of the Revisionist Betar movement. Sharon was instead the pupil of Ben Gurion and Dayan and his military ideas were the product of his years of service in Unit 101 and afterwards. Lawyers of *Time* fighting Sharon's famous libel case against the magazine called him a 'bloodthirsty, insubordinate militarist'. Like Begin he had great ambitions and, according to Zeev Schiff and Ehud Ya'ari in *Israel's Lebanon War*, [16] Sharon was 'prepared to stake the national interest on his struggle for power'. Once in office Sharon surrounded himself with like-minded men who had served with him in Unit 101: Chief of Staff Raphael Eitan and Menachem Milson, who became Civil Administrator in the West Bank. Milson had been a professor of Arabic and translator of Arabic mystical works — which did not deter him from taking on the job of pacifying the West Bank. Two other key men were Moshe Arens, Israel's Ambassador in Washington, and David Kimche, Director-General of the Foreign Ministry, formerly head of the Lebanon desk in Mossad, the counter-espionage service, who travelled with the five-man team rather than being a part of it.

Raphael Eitan was described in *The Jerusalem Post* editorial on 19 April 1983, the day of his retirement, as follows:

> Never in the nation's experience has there been a chief of staff so insensitive to the proper limits of his position, so imbued with militarist values, so alien to the liberal spirit of a democratic society as Eitan [who] genuinely believes . . . the ethos of arms to be the condition of Zionist survival . . . reducing the Zionist ideal, embalming it in the spectre of the garrison state.

Eitan's own comment on the 1982 war demonstrates his adherence to both Jabotinsky's Iron Wall and Peres' 1963 'preventive war' doctrines:

> If we hadn't gone to war they [the Syrians and the PLO] would have opened war against us in several years . . . The results [of the war] made clear to the Arab world that if they want to use force against us they will have to think about it 1000 times. [17]

Although he was not one of the architects of the Etzel War, Yitzak Shamir, Begin's Foreign Minister, loyally supported the Prime Minister to the extent of losing popular support while himself serving as Premier after Begin's resignation in 1983 and failing in the 1984 election by his continued advocacy of the Lebanon debacle. Schiff and Ya'ari call Shamir 'the most belligerent and uncompromising foreign minister in the country's history' who always 'aligned himself with the most ardent of the extremists, who supported every proposal for radical military moves'. [18] A man with a reputation for secrecy who, before his appointment as Foreign Minister in 1980, had always remained in the shadows, being the third pre-state underground leader (after Ben Gurion and Begin) to rise to political predominance in Israel. He was the operations chief of Lehi, the Stern Gang, in the triumvirate (Israel Eldad being the ideologue) which assumed control after Avraham Stern's death until the group's disbanding in 1948. Shamir spent his subsequent career in sensitive work, first with Mossad, then with the Herut Party, negotiating exit visas for Soviet Jews. In a tribute to Ben Gurion on the sixth anniversary of his death, Shamir described him as a 'stiff-necked fighter, who put not his faith in foreign princes, and who drew on the spiritual well-springs of his people to do battle'. Like Sharon he opposed the peace with Egypt, preferring to cow the Arabs rather than to make peace with them. Shamir appointed the other Mossad man, David Kimche, to his key post in the Foreign Ministry where he became the Government's official spokesman for the war.

The last of Begin's quintet was Moshe Arens,[19] posted to Israel's most important embassy a few months after the 1981 election, once Begin's war plans began to materialize. Arens' task was to convince the Reagan Administration that a war in Lebanon was inevitable. A Revisionist raised in the US who emigrated to Israel and joined the settlement of Mevo Betar which had the reputation of conducting 'private revenge missions' against Arab villages, Arens studied aeronautical engineering, then went into arms manufacture. A hawk who supported the development of Israel's nuclear war capability, Arens is no less militant than Sharon although his style is polite and unassuming.

Although there was a messianic undercurrent in Zionism and messianic politics had burst through the surface of Israeli political life, messianism — religious or nationalistic — was still regarded with suspicion by a majority of Israelis. And there was in the society, its parliament and even this most hard-line of hard-line cabinets a powerful disinclination to launch military adventures. Thus the scenario of 1956 and 1967, when the Government was propelled into war by the military and the political militarists, had to be re-enacted.

The first Begin government, 1977–81, had had some success in preparing the public psychologically for the war Begin intended to wage. By changing the official terminology for the West Bank areas occupied in 1967 from 'administered territories' to 'Judea and Samaria', the Government did induce a change in the attitude of many Israelis towards the West Bank, reinforcing their emotional attachment to the territories and their determination to hold on to them. But the society was not ready to commit itself to either a messianic settlement programme in the territories, or a messianic war in Lebanon. Therefore, Begin and his team had to resort to elaborate deceptions to achieve their internal and external political objectives. It was a team particularly suited to carrying on just such a conspiracy — against the Israeli people.

The Mechanics of the Conspiracy

Ze'ev Schiff and Ehud Ya'ari give a clear picture of how Begin's second government operated. His first had in it three experienced military men — Dayan, Weizman and Yadin — who restrained the Prime Minister, who knew very little about military matters. But,

> Ariel Sharon played exactly the opposite role in the new Cabinet, constantly chivvying the Prime Minister into taking radical steps. From the day he entered the Defense Ministry in early August 1981, Sharon strove to eliminate the traditional mechanisms that mitigated or blocked the government's natural propensity toward extremism. The delicately crafted system of checks and bal-

ances that had obtained to one degree or another in all of Israel's previous governments—largely because of the presence of ministers with military experience—was conspicuously absent in this one. Other Cabinets had always comprised ministers espousing a variety of views on defense questions, thereby providing a sense of equilibrium in the decision-making process. But in Begin's new government, for the first time in the state's history, the group of leading figures who monopolized defense and foreign affairs was monolithic in its hawkish views and its readiness to employ Israel's military power for objectives that went well beyond the country's security needs. [20]

The Four Campaigns

There were four overlapping campaigns on four fronts in this Etzel War. The first front to be opened up was on the West Bank, the second on the Golan, the third in Sinai and the fourth in southern Lebanon, all of these places being considered by various messianic schools as component parts of Eretz Yisrael.

The first campaign actually began before the election of the second Likud government, with the appointment of Raphael Eitan as Chief of Staff in 1978, but was stepped up when Sharon took office in 1981. Eitan initiated new pacification measures on the West Bank, bypassing the Labour-dominated Military Administration which had exercised absolute authority since 1967 and which, in Eitan's — and Sharon's — opinion was too soft on the Palestinians. Eitan worked with sympathetic local elements within the occupation forces and with the settler movement to create semi-autonomous local defence areas in the West Bank. Settlers were issued with unlimited supplies of arms, ammunition and explosives and assigned reserve duty in their home settlements. Eitan also issued a series of draconian orders for dealing with political activism, including prolonged curfews, expulsion, harassment, establishment of detention camps, the imposition of heavy fines, firing on civil demonstrators, the blowing up and bulldozing of houses, the punishment of parents whose children were involved in demonstrations or violent incidents. [21] The second stage of the pacification plan came on 1 November 1981, with the appointment of Menachem Milson as Civil Administrator — an act which constituted a direct challenge to the Military Administration. Milson inaugurated an interventionist policy which would remove the 'political stranglehold' the PLO was said to have over the Palestinians, allegedly enabling them to choose an alternative leadership which would respect the 'silenced majority' who, Milson thought, would support autonomy as provided for in the Camp David Agreements. The Civil Administration which Milson, a reserve colonel in the IDF, set up was hardly less military than the Military Administration — it was merely made up of other Regular Army officers who were prepared to execute Milson's new policies.

His strategy was first, to stem the flow of joint Arab funds to the PLO-dominated local authorities, then to build his own political faction through the so-called Village Leagues. The imposition of what Sharon called his 'new order' resulted in organized violent resistance through March and April 1982, with nine Palestinians and two Israelis killed, 90 Palestinians, 46 Israelis and 4 foreigners wounded. On 15 May Milson proclaimed on Israel television, in the Begin style: 'We are in the midst of a battle, the greatest political battle we have waged since 1948 . . . a battle with the Palestinians. Not a war against the Palestinians but a war against the PLO.'

The second, the Golan campaign began on 14 December with the Knesset's passage of the Golan Law extending Israeli civil law and administration to the occupied Syrian territory. Although 90 per cent of the population of the Heights had fled or been expelled when the IDF seized most of the area in 1967 or during the 1973 fighting, the mainly Druze population which had remained was fiercely independent and had maintained family and communal links with Syria. When, in January 1982, the Golan inhabitants were required to obtain Israeli identification cards the Druzes demonstrated their opposition to the region's integration into Israel. In mid-February four Druze notables were put under administrative arrest. The population went out on general strike and the military reacted by closing the area, forbidding movement into it and within it, and instituted a blockade of food and medical supplies, closing down telephone lines and reducing water and electricity supplies. The closure and blockade were only lifted in April after three harsh days of total curfew. The Druze had fought the Israelis to a stand-off.

The campaign on the Sinai front was of a completely different order of things. It amounted to a vast public relations exercise staged by the messianic militants, with the connivance of the government, to traumatize the nation over the last stage of the withdrawal from Sinai, as agreed in the Camp David Accords, and particularly over the evacuation of civilians from the illegal town of Yamit, which had been built according to the Dayan plan for the integration of the territories into Israel (adopted by the Labour Government in September 1973 as the 'Galili Protocols'). One of the curious ironies of history was that the military forces which in 1972 drove the 10,000 inhabitants — bedouin and farmers — from the Yamit locale were under the command of General Ariel Sharon, who, as Minister of Defence in 1982, ordered the IDF to evacuate Jewish settlers and bulldoze the town and the settlements established there.

Writing in the *New Statesman* the Israeli journalist Amnon Kapeliouk called the Yamit withdrawal 'one of the largest brain-washing operations conducted by the government in order to convince the Israeli people that they had suffered a "national trauma", the effect of which will be felt for generations'. He cites the general in charge of the operation, who asserted, 'Everything was planned and agreed from the beginning' with the settlers, who were supposed to dramatize the event by demonstrating their resistance.[22] As could have been expected, such a campaign was a military success, but only partially so on the public relations level, and only with those who wanted to be traumatized. Those who were either convinced that Sinai had once been part of Eretz Yisrael or believed that it was useful to modern Israel have not forgiven Begin for the withdrawal—for them the campaign was nothing but a piece of theatrical comedy, in poor taste.

The fourth and largest campaign was, of course, waged in Lebanon. It was, in the opinion of Schiff and Ya'ari, 'a natural outlet for a government now looking for opportunities to make war'. [23] It had two objectives: to drive the PLO from the country and, in connection with the West Bank, establish a 'new order'. Two staff plans — 'Little Pines' and 'Big Pines' — for the invasion of Lebanon had been prepared many months before Sharon became Defence Minister on 4 August 1981. According to former Chief of Military Intelligence Yehoshua Saguy the plans were 'on the agenda' in early 1981, which means ready for use *during* the April crisis between the Maronite Christian Phalange militiamen and the Syrian Army in Zahle in the Bekaa in which the Phalange expected Israeli armed intervention on its side. At that time Prime Minister Begin (who was also Defence Minister) and the Knesset Defence and Foreign Affairs Committee wanted to go ahead with the invasion but Saguy said, 'I was opposed, and exposed my position in every forum where it was discussed, and voiced my opinion to the Prime Minister, who accepted it and decided to do nothing.' [24]

But it is clear that Begin was merely biding his time, because *before* the peak of the Zahle crisis, he had had a meeting in Jerusalem with US Secretary of State Alexander Haig, after which Begin remarked to aides, 'Ben Gurion used to say that if you're pursuing a policy that may lead to war, it's vital to have a great power behind you.' [25] Begin obviously felt Haig, and the US, would back Israel in a new Lebanon war. Begin did not use the Zahle tension to begin his war for a variety of reasons: he did not have enough support for it in the Cabinet, weakened because of the resignations of Ezer Weizman and Moshe Dayan; there was a great deal of opposition inside the country to the war everyone expected Begin to launch once the peace with Egypt had been signed; and the Israeli withdrawal from Sinai had to be completed to cement the Camp David Agreements and keep Egypt out of the fighting.

Conspiracy to War

Once in office Sharon methodically began to set the stage for the war, which, according to Schiff and Ya'ari, he had feared Begin would launch without him. [26] Following the practice set by no less a predecessor than David Ben Gurion, Sharon effected a strategic reshuffle within the IDF General Staff. And then proceeded to short-circuit the channels of command and information by transforming the National Security Unit of the Defence Ministry into an alternative, personal general staff, with a separate situation room and computer situated in splendid isolation on the topmost floor of the Defence Ministry of Tel Aviv. He shut off the flow of information to the Cabinet and the press. [27] And he and Eitan made an alliance with Mossad, which was Israel's link with the Maronite Phalange Party and militia in Lebanon and their advocate and partner within the Israeli establishment. Just as they had created a new structure to implement their new interventionist policy in the West Bank, Sharon and Eitan had to form their own obedient structure to wage war in Lebanon. Sharon adapted the staff plans—'Little Pines' and 'Big Pines'—to his requirements and had the relevant IDF commanders review these plans without telling them which would be used. Both Major-General Avigdor Ben Gal, head of the Northern Command when Sharon took over, and Bel Gal's successor Major-General Amir Drori, who assumed the command in September 1981, understood that the 'Big Pines' plan would be implemented. And this evaluation was shared by the upper levels of the General Staff. Ben Gal, who was critical of the plan, was shunned by Sharon and sidelined until he was sent to fight the Syrians in the Bekaa.

'Little Pines' involved the eradication of the Palestinian guerrilla presence, and of the PLO infrastructure, in a 40 kilometre strip in southern Lebanon; 'Big Pines' extended to the Damascus highway and to Beirut itself which the IDF expected to enter in order to drive out the PLO — Begin's personal objective was to get 'Arafat in his bunker' — and install the Phalangist militia chief Bechir Gemayel as President of Lebanon (as Ben Gurion and Dayan had wanted to do in 1954). In order to prepare the way, Gemayel declared his candidacy in November 1981 for the Lebanese presidential election due in August 1982.

The war-makers had still one major external obstacle to get round, or over: the ceasefire along the Lebanese frontier mediated in July 1981 between the PLO and Israel by the US. Sharon and Eitan devised the tactic of reinterpreting the agreement: Israel considered all violent Palestinian action against Israel — whether conducted from Lebanese territory or elsewhere —.as a violation of the agreement. The US, the PLO and world opinion did not accept this interpretation.

Sharon and Eitan would not be deterred. So confident that the war plan would go ahead was Sharon that on 5 December he broke secrecy and told Philip Habib, the US presidential envoy who had negotiated the Israel-PLO ceasefire, then visiting Israel, that the IDF was going to invade Lebanon up to Beirut, the 'Big Pines' plan. Habib declared in strong terms that the US would be opposed to such a move.[28] On 20 December (a week after the passage of the Golan Law) Begin disclosed 'Big Pines' to the Cabinet and demanded its approval for launching a war along the lines laid out in that plan — he did *not* get this approval.

Thereafter Begin, Sharon and Eitan played a game of cat and mouse with the Cabinet. They retreated from the 'Big Pines' plan and officially took up 'Little Pines', which was more acceptable. While lobbying in the Cabinet for 'Little Pines', Sharon and Eitan prepared the IDF for 'Big Pines' and by March the operational plans were nearly ready.

The original date of the invasion was set for 17 May, but seven Cabinet ministers were opposed because they feared the Syrians would become involved and the war widen. Sharon tried to reassure them by saying that there would be no confrontation with Syria — as the area of operations under the 'Little Pines' plan was limited. Meanwhile he put 'Big Pines' before the General Staff, and by isolating the politicians from the soldiers, was able to accomplish what Schiff and Ya'ari called a 'refined variation of a putsch'[29] by taking the IDF 'outside the real control of the country's legitimate government' in order to wage Israel's first war without the support of the Israeli people.

The Government, the military and the media had always prepared the Israeli people psychologically for Israel's earlier wars — with the exception of the 1973 war, which was begun by the Arabs. Therefore, before hostilities began there was what was called a 'national consensus' in favour of military action. Although the Israeli people generally expected Begin to go to war after his re-election in 1981, and particularly after Sharon's appointment, they were apprehensive about the coming war. As tension built up in the country in the months preceding the war, the Labour opposition vigorously criticized the Begin government's warpath policy and the majority of Israelis held back approval. The Cabinet's refusal to approve the invasion on 17 May was a reflection of the mood of the country.

During a visit to Washington at the end of May, Sharon met with US Secretary of State Alexander Haig, who made two key points to Sharon: that one country could not tell another how to defend itself, and that Israel should not go too far. Sharon, ready for war, construed the Secretary's remarks as a 'green light' to go ahead. The shooting in London on 3 June of the Israeli Ambassador Shlomo Argov by anti-PLO Palestinians gave Sharon the pretext he sought to launch the invasion. But because he did not have the popular support considered necessary to launch the war or the backing of the Cabinet, Sharon had to devise a complicated scheme of multiple deceptions,[30] deceptions in which Prime Minister Begin also played a role and of which he became a victim.

War by Deception

The Cabinet was the first to be deceived and it continued to be deceived throughout the war. The assassination attempt on Argov took place on 3 June; on 4 June the Israeli airforce launched softening-up bombing raids against PLO positions in Beirut and the south, which amounted to the first action of the war. On 5 June Begin called a special Cabinet meeting at 10 o'clock at night to inform his ministers of his decision to send the IDF to Lebanon the next morning. The meeting was meant as a formality and not as an opportunity to discuss fully Israel's war aims. Sharon informed the ministers that the fighting would be over in 48 hours.

The time of the session was carefully chosen — late at night and within hours of the time the operation was set to begin. Begin and Sharon pressed for a vote and Deputy Premier Simha Erlich and Energy Minister Yitzak Berman abstained because they said they could not approve of a war without being informed of its objectives. What was considered 'proper control' was not exerted by the Cabinet until 42 hours after the invasion had begun, the limits of 'Little Pines' exceeded and the Syrians engaged in combat. And then this 'control' was imposed only after two more ministers, Mordechai Zipori of Communications and Zvulun Hammer of Education, had joined their protesting colleagues. Such 'control' as the Cabinet managed to secure was intermittent and weak. [31]

Sharon had, in the opinion of Professor Harkabi, 'a lot of latitude' because Begin knew very little about military matters and he 'was such a weak man as Prime Minister; he was not master in his own house'. Zippori, a former Deputy Defence Minister, was the only member of the Cabinet with military experience and was unable to carry the group with him in urging restraint and caution. Sharon and Eitan capitalized on this state of affairs to get approval of moves which were not fully understood, or appreciated, or to obtain *ex post facto* approval of other moves which were given military justification; or the moral justification that certain moves would save the lives of the troops. Sharon managed to keep the Cabinet one step, or several steps, behind him by imposing his own briefing pattern on it. After a day in his situation room, or at the front, he would meet the Cabinet at the magic hour of 10 p.m. to inform it of the day's happenings and give it some idea of how the war was progressing, managing as much as possible to avoid interference by the politicians.

It was clear that by Sunday 13 June, Sharon had completely succeeded in his policy of isolating the political and military establishments, one from the other. On that day the IDF joined up with its Phalangist allies and swept into East Beirut. Schiff and Ya'ari wrote that this event 'marked the transformation' of the operation 'from a limited military action . . . into a runaway war to conquer an Arab capital'. Because it had ceased to exert 'proper control', meaning effective control, over the war from its first hours, by the end of the first week the Cabinet had lost the power to intervene later on, particularly after 26 July when Sharon escalated the bombardment and tightened the siege of West Beirut. Many informed commentators, like Schiff and Ya'ari are highly critical of the Cabinet's inability to intervene. [32] But then they do not take into consideration the partnership between the civilian and military establishments and the lack of regulatory mechanisms and procedure. Previous Cabinets had achieved a *modus vivendi* with the military, even when capitulating to military diktat, as in 1967, because there had been some give and take, some will to accommodate on both sides. But Sharon had no intention of working with the Cabinet — he would only work through it, with the able assistance of that powerful and popular autocrat, Menachem Begin. For the first time in Israel's history the IDF was beyond the reach of the politicians and under the command of a man dedicated to what Schiff and Ya'ari call 'a war of deceit'. And for this 'war of deceit' Sharon put into the field an estimated 120,000 troops against some 30,000 Syrian Army troops stationed in Lebanon, who accepted a ceasefire after four days of sporadic fighting, and 12,000 PLO guerrillas, with light to medium arms, who entrenched themselves in Beirut. Thus the ratio of attackers to defenders in 1982, after the capitulation of the Syrian Army, was ten to one.

The Americans were the second to be deceived. In a letter to President Reagan, Premier Begin stated that the 'Peace for Galilee' operation would be of short duration, confined to the 40 kilometre 'security belt' in south Lebanon, and that the Syrians would not be involved. Indeed, he asked the

American President to contact the Syrian President and tell him this. And on 7 June, when the operation had already gone beyond the limits set, Begin asked the American Middle East Mediator Philip Habib to carry a similar message to Damascus.

The Syrians were third. Sharon's plan involved not only attacking Syrian troops in the way of the Israeli advance, but also surrounding the units in Beirut and expelling the Syrian Army from the whole country. But he kept deployments secret, even from his soldiers. Major-General Drori, for example, was not fully briefed on the plan, although he managed to guess, quite accurately, how it would unfold. On Saturday 5 June, a seaborne force under paratroop commander Amos Yaron put out to sea without knowing what its destination would be: it received its orders at sea to proceed to the coast opposite Damour, well north of the 40 kilometre line, with Beirut as its objective.

Premier Begin was also deceived, first and foremost about Sharon's intention to attack the Syrian missile batteries in the Bekaa Valley near the Lebanese-Syrian frontier. Sharon simply saw that the assessments Begin was given were carefully censored, then approached the Prime Minister with suitably dramatic demands for action which would stir him into acquiescing in anything Sharon wanted to do.

Above all the 'Peace for Galilee' operation deceived the *Israeli citizen soldiers* ordered into Lebanon for the first 72 hours of the war, though those deployed initially beyond the 40 kilometre limit knew they would be going to Beirut. Once the IDF was seen to be expanding the theatre of war, the soldiery, for the most part, accepted the explanation that the PLO had to be driven from Beirut and that the IDF was going there to back up the Phalangist militia which would do the job. The Phalangists, however, expected the IDF to 'liberate' the city for them and had long before made this clear to the Israeli high command.

The Creation of a National Consensus

Although they had not given their support to the idea of a war in Lebanon, the Israeli people rallied round when the war became a fact. There was *ex post facto* 'consensus': in a poll taken in the third week of the war 93.3 per cent of the sample justified the operation in 'varying degrees', 77.6 per cent were definitely in favour, 15 per cent had reservations. [33] Alignment Knesset Member Mordechai Gur (Minister of Health in the 1984 national unity government) said that the war was initially given overwhelming support because the majority of Israelis believed in a 'military solution' to the problem of the PLO, and because they believed that the exercise of military force by Israel had always been effective.

The instant popular reaction was, true to form, part atavistic, part nationalistic, and part, as an old lady on the street put it to a roving correspondent, '. . . now we have to give our boys at the front the feeling that we are all united behind them, 100 per cent!' [34] This desire to demonstrate solidarity with the troops at the front was the most important element in this reaction. The public excused the Government's most obvious lies, asserts Gur, which were 'substantive', not 'tactical'. To make the situation worse, the public 'was suspicious of the war's critics' once it had begun. Thus the leadership of the Labour Alignment, which had been critical of Begin's belligerent policies, withheld its criticism once the fighting commenced. Then on 6 June Labour leaders met with Begin and declared their 'unlimited support' for the Government in securing peace for Galilee. Gur believes that the public would not have 'trusted' Labour if it had been openly critical. But fear of adverse reaction was not the only reason for Labour's weakness: the Party was split into at least three factions — those who supported 'Big Pines' (like left-wing Mapam's Imri Ron), the majority who backed 'Little Pines', and the all-out opposition (Yossi Sarid, Mordechai Gur, who commanded the 1978 Litani Operation, and Aharon Harel, a former hawk). The consequences of Labour's failure were far-reaching, [35] as political commentator Amiram Cohen made clear:

> The Labour Party, by remaining silent and by retreating from its declared positions during the first weeks of the war, became a part of the famous 'consensus', played into Begin's hands and permitted him to carry on, as he did, with the adventure. Only when the danger rose that the IDF would enter [West] Beirut . . . did the Forum [Peres' unofficial Shadow Cabinet] and the Bureau begin to speak unequivocally — against. [36]

There were two other factors operating against open opposition to the war. The first was the deception the generality of Israelis practised on themselves: they hoped and came to believe that the Lebanese adventure would indeed radically change the course of history in their favour, that Sharon might just succeed in erasing Palestinian national consciousness by waging war against the PLO, that he might just manage to elect a government in Lebanon friendly to Israel which would conclude a formal peace agreement. The scenario for Israeli–Lebanese accord was wishful thinking to the extent of being delusion, as Schiff and Ya'ari demonstrated in their book, quoting Pierre Gemayel, [37] founder of the Phalange Party and father of Israel's candidate for the Lebanese presidency, who told his Israeli contacts that he had been 'forced' to turn to Israel which had caused him 'shame and dismay' because it has been Israel that had made the Palestinians settle in Lebanon and take up arms. An alliance with such an unwilling partner could never have been expected to be very profitable. Moshe Sharett had predicted as much in 1954: 'A vain fantasy . . . We'll get bogged down in a mad adventure that will only bring us disgrace.' [38]

The second factor was the emotional appeal of the grand scheme, of Begin's ringing slogans, 'No more katushyas on Kiryat Shmona' and 'Peace for Galilee'. Because of their Zionist education and upbringing, messianism finds some resonance in the majority of Israelis, and Begin and Sharon relied on this. This war — proclaimed the 'War for Eretz Yisrael' — was second only in messianic terms to the 1967 war. It could not but capture the imagination and enthusiasm of the majority of Israelis.

The War of Choice

But the resonances of Zionist messianism had its limits: Begin deceived himself on the receptiveness of the public to his ideas about the nature of the war Israel was fighting. Ironically it was on the issue of removing deception concerning the nature of Israel's earlier wars that the Prime Minister went too far for public opinion, and the IDF. The military men responsible for the 1982 war took the line Israel had traditionally adopted: that it had 'no alternative' but to take action against the PLO in order to secure the West Bank against the Organization's dangerous influence. All Israel's other wars had been wars of 'no alternative'. But the civilian Begin adapted Shimon Peres' 1963 concept of 'preventive war' — which must not be confused with the more respectable 'pre-emptive war' — to fit his own 'wars of choice' doctrine. Begin spoke of wars fought to cripple the Arab capacity to make war, not wars fought to pre-empt an Arab first strike, which could be wars of 'no alternative'. Begin enunciated his doctrine on 8 August during a speech to the National Defence College. He began by placing it in another life-or-death messianic context: 'A classic war of no alternative was the Second World War waged by the Allies . . . What price did humanity pay for the war of no alternative? Between 30 and 40 million killed.' But, he went on, 'Operation Peace for Galilee is not a military operation resulting from lack of an alternative. The terrorists did not threaten the existence of the State of Israel.' The operation was meant to *prevent* them from developing this capacity. Begin then went on to list Israel's three 'wars of no alternative': the 'War of Independence' (November 1947-January 1949), the 'Yom Kippur War' of October 1973 and the 'War of Attrition' of 1968-70 along the Suez Canal.

> Our other wars were not without an alternative. In November 1956 we had a choice. The reason for going to war then was the need to destroy the *fedayeen*, who did not represent a threat to the existence of the State . . . In June 1967 we again had a choice. The Egyptian army concentrations in the Sinai approaches did not prove that Nasser was really about to attack us. We must be honest with ourselves. We decided to attack him.[39]

Begin would link his war with the 1967 war — both 'wars of choice' waged by Israelis to secure Eretz Yisrael. In effect Begin was suggesting that he should be raised to the supreme level in Israeli, and Jewish, history attained by the military messiahs Ben Gurion and Dayan. But he failed miserably because the Israelis refused to accept the truth of his doctrine, because they preferred to remain deceived by their carefully construed version of history.

Sharon's Objectives

The mental preference for the doctrine of wars of 'no alternative' facilitated the transformation of 'Little Pines' to 'Big Pines'. Once Sharon had decided that Israel had 'no alternative' but to drive the PLO fighters from the south of Lebanon it was easy to expand this into the push to Beirut: Israel had 'no alternative' but to root out the PLO there and drive it from Lebanon. In Sharon's mind Tyre and Sidon and Beirut were all the same — hideouts for 'terrorists'. Schiff and Ya'ari have told the whole story: As early as October 1981, Sharon told the General Staff: 'When I speak of destroying the terrorists, it means a priori that [the operation] includes Beirut.' [40] Sharon enlarged on the scenario he had in mind before audiences of selected military personnel, but not before the Cabinet, or other civilians. He would destroy 'the terrorist organizations in Lebanon in such a way that they will not be able to rebuild their military and political base. It is impossible to do this without running into the Syrians and driving them out of Lebanon as well.' To prevent the PLO from returning, Bechir Gemayel's election to the presidency must be engineered by securing the support of 66 of the 90 deputies in the Lebanese Parliament. Such a regime would be 'legitimate', 'not a puppet government'; it would sign a peace treaty with Israel and join 'the free world'. After the PLO's expulsion from Beirut the leadership would be forced to take refuge in Damascus where it would be under close Syrian control and lose its influence in the West Bank enabling a more pliable 'moderate' Palestinian leadership to emerge there. Sharon also sought to push out the Palestinian civilians living in the Tyre and Sidon areas, and in the camps south of Beirut. The massive size and destructive force of IDF assaults were meant to dislodge the bulk of these people and drive them across the frontier into Syria from where they were expected to find their way to Jordan, which Sharon and like-minded Israelis considered to be 'the Palestinian state'. Jordan would then become the sole outlet for Palestinian political expression.

The Results of the Invasion

Of these objectives only the first was accomplished, in part. The PLO was forced to leave Beirut, but Arafat was neither taken 'in his bunker' nor forced to go to Damascus. The PLO both retained its political independence and its following in the West Bank and Gaza. The IDF forced the Syrian Army to withdraw from West Beirut, but not from the rest of Lebanon, not even from the hills overlooking the city. Although it is not absolutely clear whether or not the deceivers were deceived by their Phalangist allies on the question of the 'liberation' of Beirut, it is obvious that the deceivers felt themselves deceived over the reaction of the Lebanese President-elect to Israel's demands for political payment on his military debt.

On the night of 30 August to 1 September, Bechir Gemayel flew to Nahariya in northern Israel for his first meeting with Begin, Sharon, Eitan and Kimche.

Begin began by demanding that Bechir's first act as President should be to pay a visit to Jerusalem, or Tel Aviv, that a date should be set for the signing of a peace treaty, that the renegade Lebanese officer Major Saad Haddad should be appointed commander of the south. Bechir was furious at his treatment by the Israeli Prime Minister and refused to commit himself to anything. And on 14 September, eight days before his inauguration, Bechir was blown up by a massive bomb placed in the Phalange Party headquarters. Israel blamed Syria, and a suspect with connections with a pro-Syrian political group was duly arrested and charged; but many Lebanese, including Phalangists, believed the Israelis had killed Bechir because he had shown himself too independent. He was succeeded by his older, more moderate brother Amin, whose politics followed those of his father, Pierre, who had been reluctant to form an alliance with Israel. Amin chose instead the backing of Syria, and in the spring of 1984 abrogated the US-mediated May 1983 agreement on Israeli troop withdrawal, border security arrangements and 'normalization' of relations between Israel and Lebanon.

The Begin government was also disappointed by the Reagan Administration which did not define the 'opportunity' it was offered by Israel's military success in Lebanon in the same way as did the Israelis. They expected the US to focus on the rebuilding of Lebanon and forget about the West Bank. Reagan did just the opposite. On 2 September he announced his plan for an autonomous Palestinian entity in the West Bank which would be linked to Jordan. Begin promptly refused to consider it, without consulting his Cabinet, but because it remains on the books, it is still on the agenda of would-be peacemakers.

But dispersing the PLO leadership and fighters, establishing a 'new order' friendly to Israel in Lebanon and offering the US political 'opportunities' came a long way behind Sharon's design to reconcentrate the Palestinian population of south Lebanon and Beirut in Jordan. This was his most spectacular objective, and the one in which he most spectacularly failed. The idea that the Palestinians could be expelled from Israeli-held areas had gained currency among militant settlers in the territories during the late 1970s and caused a rise in settler violence against the Palestinian inhabitants of the territories. Messianic military men saw that intermittent settler violence would not force the Palestinians to leave and grew to believe that the recreation of the sort of 'revolutionary conditions' that had obtained in 1948-49 in Palestine would accomplish the task of clearing the Land of its unwanted inhabitants. But those in the West Bank had to be destabilized in stages: first the PLO leadership outside had to be destroyed and the PLO leaders in the territories uprooted, then the Palestinians had to be made to flee Lebanon, this people's third largest and most politically potent geographical base. Once this was accomplished, the Palestinians in the territories would be psychologically prepared to leave. The campaign against the Palestinians had the messianic goal of securing for Israel domination over the entire land.

The Campaign Against the Palestinians

The aerial bombardment of Tyre and Sidon and the nearby Palestinian camps began on Saturday 5 June, before the IDF crossed the frontier. On Sunday the IDF took up positions round Tyre and opened up with land-based artillery and the Israeli navy instituted massive bombardment of both Tyre and Sidon from the sea. On Monday 7 June, Sidon fell under the hammer of the artillery. Also on Monday, the Israeli airforce dropped leaflets telling the inhabitants of the two cities to flee to the beaches, where they were rounded up and fenced in with barbed wire so the Israelis could screen all the men.

Of the 61,000 Palestinians who lived in the five camps under heavy bombardment, many civilians stayed as the PLO had built effective shelters against the periodic air raids to which they had been subjected in 'retaliation' for Palestinian operations against Israel. And many civilians were killed in the onslaught, particularly in the largest camp, Ain El Hilweh, near Sidon, because the PLO fighters there refused to surrender and fought for six days before their positions were taken. During these six days the camp was bombarded from the air in such a way, wrote David Richardson in *The Jerusalem Post*, as to be 'systematically reduced to rubble'.[41] Then 'Israeli troops in armoured personnel carriers inched their way in behind bulldozers.' And after the Palestinian guerrillas had been killed, the bombing continued until the bulldozers were sent in to flatten what was left. After the second largest camp, Rachidiyeh, in Tyre, was taken, every third house was dynamited. According to an Israel military spokesman this was because they had 'bunkers' or 'air raid shelters', though most of the shelters were for the families who dwelt in the houses. On 23 June the United Nations Relief and Works Agency (UNRWA), which maintains the camps, reported that the smallest, Mieh-Mieh, was 'slightly damaged'; in Bourj El-Shemali 35 per cent of the houses were destroyed; in El-Buss 50 per cent of the houses and four of the major social centres were destroyed; in Rachidiyeh 70 per cent of the houses were destroyed (one-third after its occupation, as mentioned above) and Ain El-Hilweh was totally destroyed.

This campaign left 44,000 of the camp-dwellers homeless and the homes of most of the others in the four target camps damaged in varying degrees. Living in the Sidon and Tyre areas but not in the UN camps were an additional 52,000 Palestinians, many of whom joined the hundreds of thousands of Lebanese made homeless by the invasion. The Palestinian camps around Tyre and Sidon were not the only victims of such harsh treatment: two camps outside Beirut, Bourj El-Barajneh and Chatila, and the heavily Palestinian neighbourhoods, Fakhani and Sabra, were bombed from the air on 4 and 5 June, then massively bombarded from the air, sea and land from 10 June until 12 August, when the US President ordered the Israeli Prime Minister to call a halt. This area south of Beirut had a population of some 80,000, about half Palestinian and the rest Lebanese, mainly Shia refugees from the south.

The Israeli army of occupation did nothing to conceal its intentions towards the Palestinian civilians: Lieutenant-Colonel Dov Yermiya, who went to south Lebanon to supervise Israeli relief work among the civilian population, describes in his *War Diary*[42] how the local commanders at first refused to provide the population with water and food, particularly those imprisoned behind the barbed wire on the beaches, then blocked efforts of local municipal workers to restore electricity and water supplies. The Israeli Government's intentions were spelled out on 18 June by Economy Minister Ya'cov Meridor, who had just been appointed 'Coordinator of Activities for Aid and Restoration of War Refugees'. Asked by one of the participants in a conference of local military officers what the policy towards the Palestinians would be, Meridor replied, 'We have to push them (he demonstrates with a movement of his hands) eastwards towards Syria. Let them go there and don't let them return.'[43]

The Phalangist fighters, who had been beaten on the field of battle by PLO fighters between late 1975 and early 1976, were eager to assist the Israelis in this action, though they had refused to join in the fighting against the PLO in Beirut. The Phalangist militia chief Bechir Gemayel had repeatedly made public statements about pushing the Palestinians out of Lebanon, expressing a preference for sending them to Saudi Arabia where, he said, they could join their brethren in tents in the desert. Under Phalangist pressure the lame duck government of outgoing President Elias Sarkis refused to allow UNRWA to put up tents for the homeless in the bombed and bulldozed camp sites in the south. And Israel quickly imported Phalangist militiamen who established 'offices' near the camps so they could harass the Palestinians who were living in the rubble and prevent others who had fled inland from returning. Under IDF auspices the Phalangists also carried out a 'liquidation campaign' of PLO partisans in the Sidon and Tyre areas. But by mid-August international pressure on Israel and the Lebanese Government prevailed and UNRWA was able to put up tents in the camps.

The scenario was repeated, and elaborated, in West Beirut. But there the Palestinians dug in and fought for eight weeks, holding out in spite of massive air, land and sea bombardments, a siege and the blockade of food, water and electricity supplies. The aim of the assault was to drive the bulk of the Lebanese civilian population — numbering about half a million — out of West Beirut so that the IDF could move in, as it had in Tyre and Sidon, and drive out the Palestinian fighters. But four-fifths of the West Beirutis stayed put and the thrust of a last-ditch Israeli ground attack on 5 August was blunted by Palestinian guerrillas in the southern suburbs where the camps of Bourj El-Barajneh and Chatila were situated. After Israel was forced to cease its heavy bombardment of West Beirut on 12 August, the Sharonists were also obliged to accept the American-mediated PLO withdrawal from the city. As part of the package Israel had to give vocal assurances to the Americans that its army would not enter West Beirut after the PLO withdrew.

On 21 August the PLO fighters commenced their evacuation from Beirut, brandishing their arms and claiming victory in front of the world's television cameras. On the 23rd Bechir Gemayel was elected President of Lebanon under the guns of the IDF and on that day ordered a battalion of the Lebanese Regular Army into Bourj El-Barajneh, which was covered on three sides by IDF units. There the Lebanese Army made arrests. According to Schiff and Ya'ari the Phalangist officers observing the operation from a distance 'bragged of the slaughter they would visit on the Palestinians'. [44] Bechir Gemayel had made no secret of the fact that he wanted to raze the camps and bidonvilles of the southern suburbs and build parks and tennis courts along the road to the international airport. On 25 August the multinational force disembarked in Beirut to keep the peace while the Palestinians departed; when on 10 September the PLO evacuation was complete, the force was also withdrawn, although the US mediator had planned that it should remain for at least another fortnight.

During this period Sharon and President-elect Gemayel consulted on what to do next. Sharon resurrected a military operation designated as 'Moah Barzel' or 'Iron Brain' [45] from his overall plan for the assault on West Beirut, which had been *turned down* by the Cabinet on 17 July. To prepare the ground for an assault on the Sabra-Chatila area, Israeli forces crossed the ceasefire lines on 3–4 September and cleared mines from access roads to this area and set up observation posts. It was decided that the operation would take place on 24 September, the day after Gemayel's inauguration. The Phalangists would occupy the Sabra-Chatila areas on the pretext of purging them of some 2,000 Palestinian fighters — 'terrorists' — the Israelis insisted had remained behind.

But the assassination of Gemayel on 14 September caused the Israelis, and their allies, to revise their plan of action. The IDF moved quickly into West Beirut and surrounded the Sabra-Chatila neighbourhoods; then on the 16th the Phalangists were funnelled into the closed area and the slaughter began. The Sharonists and Phalangists believed that once the unprotected Palestinian civilians saw how they would fare in a Lebanon dominated by the Phalange, they would fly to Syria then Jordan. The intention was to do in Sabra and Chatila what had been done in Ain El-Hilweh in spite of the fact that the desired results had not been achieved there, or elsewhere in south Lebanon. The Palestinians stubbornly remained.

The Failure of Messianic Militarism

At every stage the Begin-Sharon team took fantastic risks — by waging a 'war of choice', drastically expanding a limited action into a full-scale war, adopting brutal tactics and relying on treacherous allies. They took these risks because they had fantastic visions of what they thought could be achieved by such a grand-scale politico-military operation. The Likud's militarists had been led astray by the messianic undercurrent of Zionist ideology: they took the risk of alienating not only Israel's allies but also the Israeli people. Support for the war began to wane within 72 hours of the IDF's invasion of southern Lebanon, particularly among the troops fighting there, because they did not see it as a *defensive war*, they objected to its expansion, they were shaken by the IDF's frontal assaults on the Palestinian camps and the open cities of Tyre and Sidon. However, the consensus favouring the war did not shift to outright opposition until after the most fantastic affront of all to Israeli sensibilities — the Sabra–Chatila massacre.

Sharon, in particular, had been warned against introducing Phalange militiamen into Palestinian majority areas. No less a person than the head of Israeli Military Intelligence, Major-General Yehoshua Saguy, made his opposition clear on 12 August during a meeting in the Defence Minster's office, described by Schiff and Ya'ari. Saguy warned that the Phalange would want to 'settle old scores . . . One day the murders will start, and they will just go on and on without end. Every paper in the world will be there to cover the extermination . . . They'll lay everything at our doorstep!' [46] And that was exactly what happened—and Israel's responsibility was clear because the IDF had sealed off the area and regulated the entry of the Phalange militiamen allegedly longing to avenge the death of their leader on any of their political foes. 'Iron Brain' could not have been more ill-conceived: it did not drive the Palestinians away; the Phalangist militia, which would have needed to follow up the massacre with further harassment to get them moving, was withdrawn and thereafter excluded from West Beirut; the press published its horrifying reports and Israel was condemned; the inquiry conducted in Israel on the affair brought about Sharon's demotion from the Defence Ministry, an abrupt end to the rule of the messianic militarists and a diminution of their influence.

This grandiose plan could not but fail. But the question must be asked. How did they expect to succeed? One has to delve into history, and Zionist mythology to find an answer. To go back only 35 years to the 'miraculous' creation of the state and to its equally 'miraculous' expansion in 1967. Chapter 2 has shown just how much painstaking effort and dedication and patience went into these 'miracles'. The men who made them were the hard-headed pragmatists of the Zionist movement. But then there were others, like Jabotinsky, who believed in hurrying miracles along by the premature use of force. These were the secular and religious messianics. Chaim Weizmann, one of the founding fathers of the state and its first President, warned against those Zionists 'seeking to live by a sort of continuous miracle, snatching at occasions as they presented themselves, and believing these accidental smiles of fortune constituted a way of life'.

Notes

1. Amos Oz quoted by Josh Gumson in 'Questions on Questions', in *New Outlook*, October/December 1983.
2. Shubert Spero contributed this important article to *The Jerusalem Post International Edition*, 24 June to 1 July 1984.
3. Reuven Alberg in *The Jerusalem Post International Edition*, 26 February to 3 March 1984.

4. Shlomo Avineri, considered a 'hawk' by such 'doves' as Meron Benvenisti, has elaborated Benvenisti's own 'two cultures' theory, focusing on the issue of the future of the territories rather than the general situation. The article quoted, one of several, was in *The Jerusalem Post International Edition*, 26 September to 2 October 1982.

5. Menachem Porush was interviewed by Abraham Rabinovich in *The Jerusalem Post International Edition*, 4-10 September 1983, on the occasion of Begin's resignation as Prime Minister.

6. Begin was quoted in *Party Politics in Israel and the Occupied Territories* by Gershon P. Kieval (Westport, Connecticut: Greenwood Press, 1983), page 141.

7. *The Jerusalem Post* 30 Zionist Congress Supplement, November 1982.

8. Yadin's role was discussed by Abraham Rabinovich in *The Jerusalem Post International Edition*, 8-14 July 1984. Yadin is lovingly portrayed, and a fictional account of just such an incident given, in *A Long Way to Shiloh* by Lionel Davidson (London: Gollancz, 1966).

9. Benvenisti is quoted by David K. Shipler in *The International Herald Tribune*, 11 July 1984.

10. Professor Harkabi has argued this case in both public meetings and the press in Israel and published in 1982 a book in Hebrew on the subject — which appeared in English in 1983 as *The Bar Kokhba Syndrome* (Chappaqua, New York: Rossel Books). In this edition he included a chapter on the Lebanon war which puts Revisionist messianism and fantasy-making into perspective. Harkabi is quoted from an article in *Koteret Rashit*, 4 July 1984.

11. Yosef Goell is quoted from *The Jerusalem Post International Edition*, 4-10 September 1983.

12.. Professor Elazar's article 'The 1981 Elections: Some Observations', appeared as a *Jerusalem Letter*, 15 August 1981, published by the Jerusalem Centre for Public Affairs, where he is editor and publisher.

13. Berman considered such a policy as being suitable only for Albania and Iran, but not for Israel which depended on both the outside world and the Jews of the Diaspora for moral, financial and military support. He resigned from the Cabinet in the aftermath of Sabra-Chatila.

14. Begin told this to Michael Elkins of the BBC who was quoted in Eric Silver's biography, *Begin* (London: Weidenfeld & Nicolson, 1984), page 182.

15. Benny Morris was quoted in *The Jerusalem Post International Edition*, 10-17 June 1984.

16. Ze'ev Schiff and Ehud Ya'ari, *Israel's Lebanon War* (New York: Simon & Schuster, 1984), page 301. This is the best book so far on the internal ramifications of the Israeli military operation.

17. Eitan is quoted from Nicholas B. Tatro in an Associated Press dispatch from Tel Aviv, 29 October 1984.

18. The article on Shamir appeared in *The Jerusalem Post International Edition*, 18-24 September 1983.

19. Arens' career was described by Shlomo Frankel in *Haolam Hazeh*, 23 February 1983.

20. Schiff and Ya'ari, op. cit., pages 38-9.

21. Dan Margalet discussed Eitan's actions in *Kol Ha'ir*, 4 March 1983, and Michael Oren wrote about the Civil Administration in 'A Horseshoe in the Glove: Milson's Year on the West Bank' in *Middle East Review*, Fall 1983, page 24.

22. Amnon Kapeliouk's article was published on 7 May 1982.

23. Schiff and Ya'ari, op. cit., page 39.

24. Saguy was interviewed by Eitan Haber in *Yedioth Ahronoth*, 19 August 1983.

25. Begin is quoted by Schiff and Ya'ari on page 31.

26. Sharon's desire to be in charge was mentioned by Schiff and Ya'ari on page 38.

27. Before Schiff and Ya'ari published their book the Israeli press produced quantities of information on how the war came about and discussed the two plans in detail. Most major papers carried multiple-page supplements on the first anniversary of the invasion; the article by Avraham Tirosh and Avi Batelheim in the *Ma'ariv* supplement was especially useful.

28. Schiff and Ya'ari cite the meeting on page 66. In May 1985 a row blew up between Ariel Sharon and the outgoing US Ambassador to Israel, Samuel Lewis, because Lewis dared to mention this meeting during an interview on Israeli television on 22 May.

29. The idea of a 'putsch' was put forward by Schiff and Ya'ari on page 58.

30. See Schiff and Ya'ari, op. cit., pages 111 ff.

31. Mark Segal produced information leaked by Cabinet sources in *The Jerusalem Post* as early as 14 June 1982, at the beginning of the war's second week.

32. See Schiff and Ya'ari, op. cit., page 181.

33. The poll conducted by the Modi'in Ezrachi Research Institute was published in *The Jerusalem Post*, 2 July 1982.

34. The correspondent was Daniel Gavron writing in *The Jerusalem Post*, 5 July 1982.

35. Eliahu Agres, director of the Histadrut daily *Davar*, described Labour's responsibility in an article in *New Outlook*, August/September 1982.

36. Amiram Cohen was writing in *Hotem*, the *Al-Hamishmar* weekend supplement, 3 September 1982.

37. Schiff and Ya'ari, op. cit., page 18.

38. Ibid., page 14.

39. The Prime Minister's military theory was published by *The Jerusalem Post International Edition*, 22-28 August 1982.

40. Sharon is quoted by Schiff and Ya'ari on pages 42-3.

41. David Richardson in *The Jerusalem Post*, 9 July 1982. According to a preliminary, and acutely controversial estimate made on 12 June by Francesco Noseda, head of the International Committee of the Red Cross, 'more than 600,000 people have been driven from their homes as a result of Israel's invasion of Lebanon'.

42. Don Yermiya, *My War Diary: Israel in Lebanon* (London: Pluto, 1984). Yermiya, retired from the IDF after a 29-year career as a professional soldier, served as a volunteer for another 15; he again volunteered to help with civilian relief operations in south Lebanon in the wake of the IDF's blitz through the cities and towns of the area. The book is an indictment of the callousness and indifference of the officers who supervised the occupation. Yermiya first published his *Diary* in serial form in the Hebrew press, then as a book, privately printed to avoid the military censors; he was expelled from the IDF as a result.

43. Quoted in Yermiya, op. cit., page 48.

44. Schiff and Ya'ari, op. cit., page 252.

45. Operation 'Iron Brain' was described by Colin Campbell in *The New York Times*, 1 October 1982.

46. Saguy's testimony is on page 250 of Schiff and Ya'ari's book. He is one of the prominent Israelis calling for an inquiry into the war.

4. The Peace Option

Militant Zionism versus a Zionism of Quality

From the moment they adopted the Basle Programme in 1897 until the proclamation of the Jewish state on 15 May 1948, the Zionists had no peace option. If Judea was to rise again it had to do so in 'blood and fire' because the Zionists had laid claim to an inhabited land. But then Zionism was a harsh creed fashioned by hard men made hard by Jewish experience. The majority never gave a thought to the people they aimed to dispossess or to how the process of dispossession would reverberate on them. Of the minority who did, some went elsewhere (like Hans Kohn) and some stayed. Those who stayed — Ahad HaAm, Martin Buber, Judah Magnes — were clear-sighted about the evil consequences for Jewish humanism of the Zionist endeavour. But they served the cause nevertheless. Perhaps it was the very egocentricity of their concern—What will this do to us?—that enabled them to promote a cause they realized would compromise their humanity. But the revival of the Jewish nation came first for them; the Palestinians were destined to be its victims. These spiritual Zionists wanted what the soldier-scholar Yehoshafat Harkabi strives for today: a Zionism of moral and ethical quality.

For Ahad HaAm, Buber and Magnes, and, much later, for Harkabi, there came a point in the conflict over Palestine where they sought to reverse the direction Zionism was taking. Ahad HaAm proposed the establishment of a model community rather than a state which would take in all the Jews; Buber and Magnes a binational state; Harkabi Israeli withdrawal from the territories occupied in 1967 and accommodation with the Palestinians. All amount to deviation from accepted Zionist ideology.

In the pre-state period the Ihud Group of Buber and Magnes was not alone in advocating a Zionist retreat from the Basle Programme. A second group which both built the Jewish homeland and tried to reverse the momentum of Zionism was the idealistic socialist Hashomer Hatzair kibbutz movement. It tried to formulate a 'progressive' Zionist ideology which could reconcile its nationalist and universalist ideals. During the violent twenties and thirties Hashomer Hatzair rejected the majority assumption that the Zionists had to change the balance of power in the country and dominate the Palestinians. The conclusion Hashomer Hatzair reached was that they should renounce the

the idea of the Jewish state and work for a just binational society in which the Jews would become a majority by immigration: a no less schizophrenic position than that adopted by the spiritualist-humanitarians. A third group was a moderate faction of the religious Mizrachi Party (which became the National Religious Party) which argued that Palestine should be partitioned between Arabs and Jews and that Jewish sovereignty should not be extended over the entirety of Eretz Yisrael by force, and certainly not through the agency of a secular nationalist state.

Finally, there were those who adopted a 'moderate' stance out of concern for *realpolitik*, who constituted (and constitute today) the majority of Israel's peacemakers. Moshe Sharett was not concerned with the soul of Zionism or with its progressive nature, and he was not religious. Like Chaim Weizmann, Sharett was a pragmatist: he was fully committed to the programme of the Jewish state in all of Palestine and was prepared to fight for it. Sharett, however, was created in Herzl's mould rather than that of Jabotinsky. He believed that Zionism's, and Israel's, actions must be moderated by consideration of external political realities: Sharett, and Weizmann before him, did not seek to antagonize Britain or chance the goodwill of the US. Sharett was not concerned over the rights and destiny of the Palestinians; he simply wanted peace and neighbourly relations with the Arab states and was prepared to pay a price for these things. The price he proposed was that the Palestinians should be compensated and Israel should renounce its claim to the portion of Palestine which remained in Arab hands. This too constituted a serious deviation from Zionist ideology and threatened to force the Ben Gurion clique to reduce their expectations. It was an option both the Syrian[1] and Egyptian regimes considered until Ben Gurion and the military swept it aside in their drive for territory.

Paradoxically, the conquest in 1967 of the rest of Palestine revived the peace option, while at the same time producing the Land of Israel Movement. The peace option was taken up by a broadly based front comprising both spiritualist-humanitarians who abhorred Israeli dominion over the inhabitants of the occupied territories and moderate pragmatists who felt that the captured lands could, in the words of Rael Jean Isaac, be 'the vehicle for finally achieving peace; the war thus became an unexampled opportunity for abruptly reversing past trends'.[2]

The peace front did not initially attract military and civilian personalities comparable to the stellar collection who supported the rival Land of Israel Movement: returning hard-won land to the Arabs did not set up the resonances in Israeli society that conquest and dominion did. But the reverse was true as far as the Diaspora was concerned because the majority of Jews there were politically liberal and against military occupation. Aware of the importance of the constituency in the Diaspora, the peace front launched information campaigns in America and Europe to counter those of the Israeli Government and the World Zionist Organization. One of the specific aims of the peace front was to make the Diaspora Jews aware that their contributions to the WZO-affiliated charities were being used to construct settlements in the occupied territories. The peace front's efforts constituted a rival Zionist campaign to 'capture the communities'.

The Zionism of the three general groupings propelled by moral considerations had a messianic aspect: Israel had not been created in the image of other nations and must not behave like them; Israel must be 'a light unto the nations'. And it had a certain pragmatism: the world had given its sympathy to Israel because of the expectation that Israel would be 'righteous'; in purely practical terms Israel could not afford to lose the moral and financial support such sympathy produced.

The peace front drew members from the traditional spiritual constituency in the universities, particularly the Hebrew University (where the Ihud Group had been based); from the idealistic youth of the left-wing Mapam Party and the Hashomer Hatzair kibbutzim (who formed the 'New Left') and from the moderate minority within the National Religious Party, notably Moshe Unna, a Member for the NRP in Israel's first six Knessets. In 1975 these NRP doves established their own organization, 'Oz VeShalom', 'Peace and Strength', to act as a counterweight to the militant settlers group Gush Emunim which, according to Yeheskel Landau, the Oz VeShalom spokesman, has 'distorted the message of Zionism and Judaism . . . by stressing militant messianism and the rights of Jews' to the exclusion of the rights of others. The group is critical of Gush Emunim's 'tendency to justify unethical behaviour by the use of Biblical rationale and its elevation of the borders of Israel over the Tora'. (See Appendix.)

The most notable activist in the front was, and is, Professor Yeshayahu Leibowitz, a distinguished organic chemist and biochemist at the Hebrew University, editor of several volumes of the *Encyclopaedia Hebraica* and writer on Jewish philosophy. He synthesized the ideology of the front, drawing from the different doctrines of the component groups. First, he argued against the annexation of the occupied territories because such action would dilute the Jewishness of the state; second, he contended that the continuation of the occupation would do great moral damage to Zionism and Israel; third, he spoke out against injustice to the Palestinians because of the Israeli domination of the territories; fourth, he said that a secular state which did not recognize the authority of the Tora, nor ensure its observance, had no right to use '"halachic" arguments'[3] to justify Israel's retention of the territories. Liebowitz's stature and persistence have made him the conscience of Israel and, in turn, have given the cause he has espoused a moral force it would never have attained without him.

Taking into account the fact that the three broad constituents of the peace front are differently motivated, it is not surprising that they have not been able to formulate a common plan for the return of the territories, though they agree that Israel's retention of those lands is an affront to Zionist values, whatever the variety of Zionism. Some, the marginals, put forward a proposal for the establishment of a Palestinian state in the West Bank and Gaza and called for the abrogation of one of the basic tenets of Zionism, the 'Law of Return' which asserts that any Jew 'returning' to Israel would be received as a citizen of the state. Such an act, they argued, would convince the Arabs that Israel had no expansionist ambitions and encourage them to make peace. Others, also marginals, reverted to the democratic binational solution. The least compromising, least moderate, and the largest, faction said that the territories should be given autonomy in federation with Jordan and criticized the settlement programme but remained vague about what should be done about the settlers already in place. Rael Jean Isaac said that in its own estimation the peace front considered 'it had the support of perhaps 5 per cent of the Israeli public,' [4] and even this support was for what was seen as the most moderate section of the front. The marginal groups were considered outside the Zionist consensus — renegades even — and only prejudiced the public against the front.

The Peace Option

Between 1967 and 1977 the peace front neither attained the minimum unity required nor formulated a plan of action to become an effective counterweight to the Land of Israel Movement which had an ideology, public support, a plan of action and a government bound by both its adherence to Zionist ideology and coalition agreements with the National Religious Party to implement it. The Land of Israel Movement had the much easier task because it operated within a closed Zionist circle while the peace front had to find Palestinian or Arab partners who were prepared for a dialogue in preparation for joint endeavour.

Then in 1977 the unequal equilibrium between the annexationist and peace forces was destabilized by the visit to Jerusalem of President Sadat of Egypt. For the first time ordinary Israelis realized that peace with the Arabs was within the realm of possibility — at a price. Sadat's price was the return to Egypt of all occupied Sinai and the opening of negotiations on the future of the occupied Palestinian territories. Begin agreed to pull Israel out of Sinai, although he hoped to keep certain areas for 'security' reasons and, even, retain the settler town of Yamit. Sadat demanded total withdrawal and got it: Begin was determined to achieve a separate peace with Israel's most powerful antagonist in order to prepare the way for what Meron Benvenisti called the Prime Minister's 'single-minded struggle for Greater Israel.' [5]

Even while the negotiations were going on, the Settlement Department of the Jewish Agency was preparing its first plan to settle increasing numbers of Jewish civilians in the West Bank and Gaza in order that permanent Israeli rule would be ensured. The 1978 settlement plan was devoted to the creation of many small outposts populated by nationalist and religious messianics — in imitation of early pioneering settlements — to lay claim to biblical lands. Quite rightly, members of the peace front and other Israelis excited by the prospect of peace with Egypt saw Begin's settlement scheme as a threat to the negotiations. In the spring of 1978, 350 officers and soldiers sent a letter to Begin critical of his annexation policy which, they argued, prevented Israel from establishing 'normal relations' with its neighbours. Stating that security could only come through peace, they warned that 'the strength of the Israel Defense Forces lies in the identification of its soldiers with the course of the state of Israel'.

Peace Now

A 'groundswell of popular support' for this letter led to the creation of 'Peace Now' (see Appendix), which staged mass demonstrations during the Camp David talks urging Begin to compromise. Calling themselves 'sane Zionists' and dedicating themselves to 'a long struggle . . . over the future of the territories', Peace Now proposed a peace plan based on the following principles: repartition of 'the land of Israel', recognition of 'Israel's right to sovereign existence' and of 'the right of the Palestinians to a national existence', security arrangements for Israel, the continuation of Jerusalem as a unified city and Israel's capital. [6] Peace Now demands that Israel should take the initiative and be ready to negotiate with 'those representatives of the Palestinians who recognize negotiations as the only path towards resolution of the conflict'. The operative part of the programme includes a moratorium on settlement and land expropriation in the West Bank, restraining the settlers, removal of restrictions on the Palestinians and safeguarding their interests, and redirection of resources channelled into the West Bank to needy areas in Israel. The main objective is to take Israel out of the state of permanent war with its neighbours. [7] The group's main supporters were initially, and have remained, men of military age, reservists and their families, professionals, intellectuals, the middle class, Ashkenazi, from various party backgrounds, ranging in age from late twenties to mid-forties. Apart from the age difference, the composition of Peace Now is comparable to that of the Land of Israel Movement eleven years earlier. But the Land of Israel Movement represented the centre-right of the old Zionist establishment while Peace Now consists of the centre of the new Israeli establishment. The ideology of the former was backward-looking and fundamentalist; Peace Now looks towards a peaceful future for Israelis in the region in which they live. The challenge the peace front faces is daunting because it must not only strive to counter the specific annexationist policies of the governments of the day, but also to halt and reverse the messianic momentum of a century of Zionist endeavour in Palestine.

Almost as soon as the American-mediated Camp David Accords were signed in March 1979 it became clear that the Egyptians and Americans differed with the Israelis on the future of the occupied territories after the five-year period of Palestinian autonomy during which the question of sovereignty was suspended. Prime Minister Begin said that Israel would neither agree to the establishment of an independent Palestinian state on the West Bank nor to hand back the territory to Jordan. Instead the Likud envisaged a division of administrative functions between Jordan and Israel and unfettered Jewish settlement throughout the area, preventing any repudiation of the Land. The Camp David Accords made settlement all the more urgent and conferred on the settlers the status of 'an arm of the State'.

The Struggle for Possession of the Territories

The first Jewish Agency settlement plan required the expropriation of Palestinian-owned land and increased tension in the territories. Then disturbances erupted in Hebron, the most conservative and fundamentalist Muslim town in the West Bank, because of the attempts by militant settlers to establish themselves in the heart of the commercial area. The Palestinians were joined in their opposition by Israelis from the left wing of the peace front. The Likud government was forced to recognize that the Palestinian resistance had a small but committed Israeli partner. Six settlers were killed by Palestinians outside a building where they had squatted illegally for a year and the Mayor of Hebron, Fahd Kawasmeh, a Muslim judge and the Mayor of nearby Halhoul were expelled from the West Bank. The low-key demographic struggle had escalated into a guerrilla campaign.

The appointment in 1978 of Raphael Eitan as Army Chief of Staff signalled a hardening of policy toward Palestinian demonstrators and a lessening of control over the settlers. As soon as he took office Eitan began to lay the foundation for the 'new order' in the West Bank which was officially proclaimed after Sharon became Defence Minister in 1981. Eitan incorporated the settlers into local 'Extended Defence Units' which were supposed to be under the IDF area command but instead organized the settlers into paramilitary units independent of authority. These units soon began to act on their own initiative against Palestinian demonstrators or to plot against their Palestinian neighbours. Their first operation took place in April 1980 and involved an attack against Palestinian property, the smashing of the windows of 120 cars and 70 houses, an incident which was locally referred to as 'Kristalnacht', recalling the night in November 1938 when Nazi thugs smashed Jewish windows and synagogues throughout Germany. The second operation was against personalities, the placing of bombs in the cars of three Palestinian mayors, two of whom were severely wounded.[8]

The peace front reacted in a variety of ways: some groups demonstrated in the West Bank alongside Palestinians; IDF soldiers on duty in the West Bank submitted formal complaints against others for brutality towards Palestinian detainees; some groups produced information material on what was happening and sent it to Zionist groups in the Diaspora in the hope that they would put pressure on the Israeli Government to curb the extremists.

The deteriorating security situation in the territories set off warning lights in the minds of many previously uninterested Israelis at the centre of the political spectrum. As a result the peace front, particularly Peace Now, began to gain the sort of passive support among certain sections of the population that only the Land of Israel Movement had previously enjoyed. This constituency was augmented by the actions of the second Begin government which increased repression in the West Bank and caused increased settler violence and the revolt of the Golan Druse.

Consensus Politics

Once Sharon became Defence Minister some of the less hawkish elements in the Labour Alignment as well as members of the Sheli and Shinui parties and the Citizens' Rights Movement made common cause with the peace front against the war everyone saw coming. In the six months between Begin's disclosure of the 'Big Pines' plan to the Cabinet and the invasion, the consensus against the war grew, and caused its postponement. Once he felt he had the acquiescence of the Reagan Administration — particularly after Sharon's visit to Washington in late May — Begin went ahead. As far as Israeli public opinion was concerned, he gambled on history: all of Israel's previous wars had the overwhelming support of its people and Begin took the chance that they would support his war as well. His gamble paid off initially because as soon as the IDF crossed the Lebanese frontier the Israelis swung behind the war front, and the Government. But this initial surge of support later sharpened the divisions and deepened the rift in the society. It became clear, within days of the invasion's outset, that the consensus was false, because the society behaved uncharacteristically when faced with the challenge of this war: dissatisfied workers continued to strike, few volunteers came forward to take up the jobs (even in hospitals and social centres) left by men sent to the front, both civilians *and soldiers* openly criticized the campaign and castigated Sharon, whom they held responsible. No longer could those within the previously sanctified security sector act with impunity.

The Anti-war Movement

The first demonstration against the war came from outside the consensus on 5 June, as the Israeli airforce bombed Beirut and the southern cities in preparation for the next day's land attack. More than 2,000 demonstrators joined a protest rally in Tel Aviv organized by the Committee for Solidarity with Bir Zeit against the 15 years of occupation of the territories — and the bombing of Lebanon, which had begun on the fourth. As a result of this rally the Committee Against the War in Lebanon (hereafter CAWL) was established (see Appendix). On 7 June the leftist student organization CAMPUS from the Hebrew University held two demonstrations against the war, one outside the Prime Minister's office, one on the university campus. On the 8th a protest watch organized in Tel Aviv by the CAWL was attacked by pro-war elements.

The opposition also took to the pages of the daily papers, publishing advertisements on 7, 8 and 9 June, and calling the invasion a 'catastrophe', a 'violation' of the 1981 ceasefire agreement and 'unnecessary'. On the 11th

Ha'aretz published an advertisement calling for 'immediate ceasefire' and withdrawal from Lebanon. On the 14th the CAWL and various women's organizations demonstrated outside the Prime Minister's office. On the 21st four distinguished intellectuals and literary figures—Professor Leibowitz, Dan Miron, Israel's foremost literary critic, Nathan Zach, its most popular poet, and Asa Kasher, a professor of philosophy from Tel Aviv University—held a press conference to call for an end to the war and the occupation. Like the CAWL and CAMPUS they opposed the war from the start, which did not amount to mass opposition—that came later.

The first large protest meeting was held in Tel Aviv by CAWL; it served to test the waters of public opinion for the more cautious sections of the peace front, like Peace Now. The rally was an unexpected success as some 20,000 people attended; the demand was for an end to the war and negotiations with the Palestinians. A spokesman in uniform read out a petition signed by 100 armoured corpsmen who had just been released from duty. The petition stated that there was no consensus favouring a military solution to the political problem of the Palestinians. The presence of fighting men in this first mass anti-war rally set the tone of the whole summer's protest and stepped up the pace of the development of the opposition movement. Thereafter it was soldiers, returning from Lebanon, and reservists awaiting their call-up, who played a major part in anti-war activities.

The soldiers made the change from backing the limited 'Peace for Galilee' operation — the 'Little Pines' plan — to opposition to the whole enterprise within 72 hours of the beginning of the invasion because, unlike the civilians at home, they could see with their own eyes the expansion of the war beyond what was generally considered a justifiable action to drive the 'terrorists' back from the northern border of Israel. Despite the fog of Government propaganda the press realized what was happening quite early on. On the 11th *The Jerusalem Post* ran an editorial entitled 'Time to call a halt' which said that Sharon's 'quest for total victory' and his attempt to 'solve' the Palestinian problem by war were 'illusions' and demanded an Israeli ceasefire. The success of the CAWL demonstration in Tel Aviv and the growing opposition in the press encouraged Peace Now to try to take its mass following into the streets. But first, on 17 June, the group published an opposition advertisement in *Yedioth Ahronoth*; then on 7 July Peace Now filled the central square of Tel Aviv with 100,000 demonstrators.

The Soldiers' Protest

With the first relays of returning soldiers came the first organized, purely military protests. These focused on specific IDF grievances against the Government and Sharon. The first group to emerge was 'Soldiers Against Silence', which condemned the Government's lying propaganda about the course of the war, particularly its involvement of the Syrians. One piece of disinformation on which they seized was a statement that the crusader castle of Beaufort, a Palestinian stronghold, had been taken 'without any killed from our forces' — which was blatant lie.

The second group to emerge had no name and no structure; it was also made up of returning reservists who, on their own, mounted a vigil outside the Prime Minister's office in the fourth week of the war which went on for 14 months, day after day, the men living in tents or camping out in the open. They demanded an end to the war and the dismissal of Sharon. The issues — beyond the lies — which gripped them were the lack of a defined military objective and of an obvious enemy ('I started to wonder how you tell a terrorist from a civilian!'), the fact that it was a 'war of choice' they were fighting rather than a war of 'no alternative' and the realization the Palestinian problem could not be solved 'with Sharon's methods'. The conclusion many soldiers had reached was put into words by an anonymous paratrooper at the end of June: 'My personal feeling . . . was that this time those sitting at the top wanted war, being totally insensitive to the price paid by the army, by the soldiers and the whole nation.' [9] During this vigil they posted the cumulative total of Israeli soldiers killed in Lebanon on a board in numbers large enough to be read by the Prime Minister in his office: many Israelis believe that this protest more than any other undermined Begin's confidence in the war, and in himself, precipitating his resignation in September 1983.

The third soldiers' group had an impact beyond its size on the morale of the IDF and the public acceptance of military service. On 8 July, a group of 86 reserve soldiers and officers, just released from duty, sent a letter to the Prime Minister and Defence Minister saying that 'there is no consensus for the war', asking not to be sent to Lebanon and demanding IDF withdrawal. [10] Their slogan became their name: 'Yesh Gvul!', 'There is a limit!' Their letter of request hardened into refusal to serve in Lebanon and, for some, in the occupied territories as well. In August the Army began to prosecute and imprison those who refused service in Lebanon. Most who signed the demand were reservists but there were a few conscripts as well. According to Eli Gozansky, a conscript signatory who served 56 days in prison, few conscripts refused to serve because they had not thought about the issues involved in the war; those who did were politically committed before entering the IDF (like Gozansky himself who is a Communist). This was not true for the majority of reservists who courted prison by refusing to go to Lebanon: they were converted by what they saw there, the destruction of the camps and of Tyre and Sidon, the conditions in which the Palestinians were living. These soldiers objected to the 'political character' of a war they saw as 'unnecessary'. The refusenik who attracted the most publicity was Reserve Private Daniel Timerman, son of the Argentine-Israeli journalist Jacobo Timerman, whose highly critical war diary, *The Longest War*, was published while the IDF besieged Beirut.

Yesh Gvul was a complete reversal of the Israeli tradition of volunteering for war service. Although fewer than 200 soldiers carried their refusal to the point of going to gaol, 3,000 signed the protest and another 4,000 support the group. On the first anniversary of the invasion Yesh Gvul formed a movement among conscripts about to join the Army. This was called 'Ad Kan', 'This Far', and it began with 250 signatories. Yesh Gvul's influence is far greater than its members would suggest because the publicity given to each of the gaoled soldiers had lent the refusal phenomenon both credibility and respectability, encouraging an estimated 25,000 soldiers to avoid service in Lebanon, and the West Bank, by appealing to their officers, inventing ailments and obtaining psychiatric referral (which before this war was considered a shameful resort) and just not appearing for their call-up.

During June and July a shoal of letters and petitions poured into the Prime Minister's office; notable among them were letters from 35 members of the élite unit which had participated in the Entebbe raid and from Avraham Burg, the son of the serving Minister of Interior and Police. Then in early August came the individual act which shocked the politico-military establishment, the resignation of his commission as commander of an armoured regiment by Colonel Eli Geva, an outstanding officer and son of a reserve general. In April young Geva had expressed his doubts about such a war which would draw in the Syrians. On this occasion, a meeting between Sharon and divisional and brigade commanders, Geva warned, 'Everything possible must be done to avoid unnecessary wars. We should fight only when there is absolutely no choice.' [11] In August Geva made it clear that he would not order his troops into Beirut because it would cause too much harm to the civilian population and inflict too many casualties on the men under his command.

Civilian Protest

The military protest merged with civilian opposition through the parents of soldiers killed or wounded in action or on active service in Lebanon. Initially angered, like the soldier' group, by the lies being told about casualties and the changing objectives and expansion of the war, they began modestly at the end of June with a demonstration, calling themselves 'Parents Against Silence', then expanded their activities to take out advertisements in the press and to join the soldiers' vigil outside the Prime Minister's office.

'Women against the War in Lebanon', formed in Jerusalem after the first CAWL demonstration, called for a protest meeting, after three weeks of fighting, in the centre of Jerusalem: it was attended by 300 women, many of whom had never before participated in such an activity, and, in the words of Aurora Jacob, one of the organizers, the demonstration was met 'with insulting and sexist abuse' from passers-by. But the effect of such a protest at home had a great impact on the soldiers at the front. A paratrooper who had served in Lebanon during the first two weeks of the war said of this particular protest: 'One of our best moments was when we heard about the anti-war demonstration of the 300 women in Jerusalem.' There was a feedback from war front to home front, then the reverse, until the anti-war movement gained the momentum it needed to have an impact on the dithering politicians, particularly on the Labour Alignment, which only dared to offer criticism when it saw that it would have a fair amount of public support.

The anti-war activities of the kibbutz movement, a key state institution, encouraged Labour to voice its opposition. Kibbutzniks participated in the big CAWL rally in Tel Aviv and in Peace Now demonstrations, and wrote collective letters to the Government, like this one: 'We, members of Kibbutz Gazit and Israeli citizens, call upon the government to observe a ceasefire on all fronts and to stop military actions in Beirut . . . The Palestinian problem, which is the actual root of terrorism, will not be settled by force but by recognition of the right of self-determination of all peoples in the region'. Then after a year and a half of participating in the demonstrations of others, the kibbutzim mounted their own effort outside the Prime Minister's office every Sunday, during the weekly Cabinet meeting, two or three kibbutzim organizing the protest on each occasion.

But all this anti-war activity did not produce a decisive popular swing against the war, and the Government. Taking into account a built-in bias in favour of the war (because respondents want to be thought patriotic) a poll taken between 10 and 19 August, when the bombardment of West Beirut reached a climax, indicated that 80 per cent of the sample still backed the war and would have done so even if they had been aware of the outcome and cost beforehand. Of the sample 64 per cent supported the campaign beyond the 40-kilometre security zone; 46 per cent were for entering West Beirut. If elections had been held during this period the Likud would have received 66 seats in the Knesset, a clear majority, and Labour only 35. This was a gain of seven seats over what the Likud would have received in June, according to another poll, amounting to a substantial improvement over the Likud's actual performance in the 1981 election, which gave it 48 seats against Labour's 47.

The Withdrawal of Public Support

The dramatic withdrawal of public support from the war, and the Likud, only came after the Sabra–Chatila massacre which took place between 16 and 18 September (Schiff and Ya'ari hold that the killing went on until the morning of the 19th). Once the news of the massacre broke, the Government was assailed from every quarter. The public demonstrated in Jerusalem and Tel Aviv; and the police brutally attacked the protestors. Then the press weighed in, in the first editions after Yom Kippur, on Monday 20 September. Ze'ev Schiff was brutally blunt in *Ha'aretz*: 'In the refugee camps of Beirut a war crime was committed.' Again in *Ha'aretz*, Eliahu Salpeter: 'One thing should be clear to all: anyone who agrees with the action of his government must bear responsibility for their results, however grave.' Hanna Zemer in Davar: '. . . the Government of Israel, which ordered the Israeli Army into West Beirut, is responsible for this slaughter.' An editorial in *Al-Hamishmar*: '. . . our hands are stained with the blood of the women and children and elderly who were slaughtered in the alleys of the camps in Beirut. With this massacre, the war in Lebanon has become the greatest tragedy to befall the Jewish people since the Holocaust.' The highly respected Yitzak Navon took an unprecedented step for the Israeli President by denouncing the massacre and calling for a commission of inquiry.

The outcry grew louder after the Cabinet meeting on 21 September because of the obstructive and dismissive attitude of the Prime Minister, and his ministers' refusal to constitute a commission of inquiry. Begin was quoted as saying, '*Goyim* [non-Jews] kill *goyim*, and they immediately come to hang the Jews,' silencing, for the moment, his colleagues and securing their approval of his communiqué which stated that 'all the direct or indirect accusations that the Israel Defence Forces bear any blame whatsoever for this human tragedy in the Chatila camp are entirely baseless and without foundation.' But the press exposed the facile lies told by Begin, Sharon and Eitan, and this time the exposure stuck, as it had not done until the massacre. On Wednesday 22, after Begin quelled a rebellion within his party's ranks and defeated a Labour motion in the Knesset to set up a state inquiry, Liberal Minister Yitzak Berman, who had opposed the war at the outset, resigned. Menachem Milson, Sharon's West Bank Civil Administrator, also resigned, and on Thursday 23, General Amram Mitzna, director of Israel's largest military college, asked to be relieved of his duties because of 'recent events' in Beirut. (He decided to stay on once the commission of inquiry was appointed.) On the 24th the Cabinet met once again under pressûre from the small Oriental Tami Party and the National Religious Party (which threatened to withdraw from the coalition their nine necessary seats) and agreed to establish an *ad hoc* commission of inquiry which would not have all the powers of judicial inquiry, as provided for in a 1968 law. The climax of the crisis came on the 25th. The Labour Party, Mapam, Shinui and Peace Now organized a demonstration in Tel Aviv which brought 350-400,000 people into the streets. It was the largest mass protest rally ever held in Israel: Begin demonstrated his inability to see reality by dismissing it as Labour's disloyalty during wartime.

But this was not the only protest demonstration. There were others: religious Jews in front of the Grand Synagogue in Jerusalem, North African Jews in Tel Aviv, soldiers, women, the Oriental neighbourhood 'Citizens Who Care' group, the Bar Association, citizens' rights groups, academic staff at universities and research institutes, the Holocaust Survivors Association. Numerous petitions were printed in the press. The message was not confined to the Government's connivance in the massacre: it was a broadside against the Likud's policies — the war, repression on the West Bank, the settlements and heavy expenditures in the territories, Begin's negative reaction to the Reagan Plan and the attempt to use military means to solve the political problem of the Palestinians.

The overt protest in the streets was matched by covert protest, amounting to 'near-mutiny', within the IDF high command. [12] While the Government dithered, more than 100 officers, all brigadiers and above, held a secret meeting in Tel Aviv during which Sharon's resignation was demanded because of his attempt to shed responsibility for the massacre by blaming the Army. (And this 'near-mutiny' was repeated in August 1983, this time forcing the Government, and its new Defence Minister, Moshe Arens, to pull the IDF out of the Chouf Mountains and redeploy along a new line on the Awali River.)

On 28 September the Cabinet established a full commission of inquiry in accordance with the 1968 law. The stubborn Prime Minister had been compelled to accede to the wishes of the people, who had come to resent the way Israel had been propelled into a war by deceit and demagoguery. A *Jerusalem Post* poll taken between 15 and 25 September (just before and just after the massacre) showed the Likud's popularity drop, estimating that it would have had 64 seats before the massacre and 60 afterwards.

But political uproar and a dip in the Likud's popularity were not the only results of the massacre. A number of new groups appeared in the peace front. The most striking of those was 'Netivot Shalom', 'Paths to Peace', founded on the same three pillars as Gush Emunim — 'the Land of Israel, the People of Israel and the Tora of Israel'. Like the earlier Oz VeShalom, it was critical of Gush Emunim for its elevation of the Land above the other two pillars. Devoted to the principle of the retention of the 'Whole Land of Israel', in practice Netivot Shalom said that Israel must be prepared to make territorial compromises for peace; wars like that in Lebanon were not considered the correct way for Israel to secure peace. The group was influential because it drew its membership from among the dozen 'hesder yeshivot', seminaries which provided both religious and military training to Orthodox Jews, their members usually comprising certain armoured units in the IDF. A second organization founded in the aftermath of the massacres was 'East for Peace'. This was established by a group of intellectuals of Oriental origin in an attempt to counter the violent image the Oriental supporters of the Likud had given to the community. The objective of East for Peace was the integration of Israel into the region: to achieve this the IDF must withdraw from Lebanon and the Government settle with the Palestinians. Such integration would enable the Oriental Jews to preserve their culture against the Western Ashkenazi, and Yiddish, culture that predominates in Israel.

Cleansing the National Conscience

The Kahan Commission report released on 8 February 1968, was from the outset a political not a judicial inquiry. Instead the chief priority of the report was to refurbish Israel's self-image: as President Yitzak Navon put it, 'We want to cleanse our conscience.' It was mandatory that the report accomplish this for a majority of those afflicted with guilt over Israel's role in the killings and beset by doubts about the character of their army. One of the three commissioners, Major-General (Reserve) Yonah Efrat had risen to head the Central Command of the IDF. The object of the inquiry was to get Israel off the moral, ethical hook, to clear the IDF of *direct* responsibility, and to restore the image of the Government as being one which was responsive to the demands of the people — even though Begin had done his best to obstruct the creation of the commission and the Likud and its supporters proclaimed opposition to its report even before it was issued. B. Michael, writing in *Ha'aretz* at the time the report was released, was correct when he said that the three commissioners were applying standards of a different era in making their assessment, the era of judicious and modestly militaristic Labour governments rather than that of the adventurist messianic militarists.

Allocating responsibility and making recommendations, the commission criticized the Prime Minister and called for the dismissal of the Defence Minister who, it said, 'bears personal responsibility', and of the Director of Military Intelligence, General Saguy (who evidently did not insist forcibly enough that Israel should steer clear of involvement with the Phalange), and the retirement of the Chief of Staff on completion of his term of service in April 1983. *Ha'aretz* editorialized on the day of the report's release: 'Whoever reads the report . . . cannot conclude that it was "too harsh", not with the military nor with the political echelon.' But, stated *Davar*, 'It is disturbing that there are still people who question why it was necessary to have an inquiry commission at all, or why the commission had to draw such severe conclusions against people of such worth, and people with such a glorious past.'

Begin refused to dismiss Sharon, who would not resign. Peace Now demonstrated for the 'immediate implementation of the recommendations' outside the Prime Minister's office on the 8th, and on the 9th there were skirmishes between Peace Now demonstrators and Sharon supporters in Tel Aviv. On the 10th Peace Now led the demonstration which ended with the killing of Emil Grunsweig. Begin implemented the letter of the commission's recommendations but not the spirit: Sharon was not removed from the Government but shifted from the Defence Ministry and retained as Minister without Portfolio. Thus the political impact of the recommendations was minimized by the very people whom they were supposed to penalize. Begin adroitly managed to keep Sharon and neutralized the protest. Israelis who had hoped that Labour would use this opportunity to attack the Government were disappointed, as were members of the peace front who had hoped that the report would change Israel's policy on Lebanon, the settlements and negotiations with the Palestinians. But then a change of policy had never been the aim of the commissioners.

Conflict of Cultures

The Peace Now demonstration on 10 February was another watershed in Israel's development. According to Shulamit Hareven, on whose description of the demonstration the account which begins this book was based,[13] what happened between Monday the 8th and Thursday the 11th made those the 'most critical days faced by Israeli democracy'. It was during this time that the lines of battle were formed between the two sections of the society, representing the two world views described as 'cultures'. Participants in this demonstration came from all sections of the peace front — the Ashkenazi intellectual élite, the Army, the neighbourhood groupings from the Oriental slum areas of Jerusalem, schools, Netivot Shalom and Oz VeShalom (who wore the same knitted skullcaps as did the supporters of Sharon). Rerservists, Orientals and the men from the religious seminaries were the particular target of the organized toughs, who branded all of the demonstrators as 'Ashkenazis'.

'The throwing of the grenade was not the most terrible thing that happened . . .' asserts Raya Harnik, mother of the major commanding the Beaufort attack who was killed during the assault. 'We went through the city . . . with people on all sides abusing us, spitting, swearing, hitting . . . without police protection'. It was the naked hatred of the counter-demonstrators that terrified and shocked the general public. Editorialists laid the responsibility squarely on the Government: '. . . and that is what was to be expected. Instead of immediately adopting the report . . . and all its recommendations, it gave time to all the [opposition] elements to organize,' said *Ha'aretz* on the 11th, which, perhaps, was the intention. Interior Minister Burg called the grenade-throwing a 'warning'. But then he was to blame for the inadequacy of police protection and the unwillingness of those who were there to restrain the counter-demonstrators.

The murder of Emil Grunsweig galvanized the peace front and alerted the public to the menace of violent messianism and blind nationalism as the Kahan Commission report never could have done. And the murder delivered a shock to the Begin government which came as the Likud's popularity was falling, a jolt which accelerated the downward slide brought on by a collapsing economy. This slide was shown in a PORI poll published in *Ha'aretz* on 28 December 1983. The question put was: 'Taking into account everything the Lebanon war has entailed — the price Israel has paid and the results it has achieved — was it, *all told*, right or not right to launch the war as it was launched?' In July 1982, 84 per cent had replied that it had been right, 13 per cent not right: in December, 64 per cent right, 32 per cent not right; in May 1983, 51 per cent said it had been right, 44 per cent not right; in November, 43 per cent said it had been right, 51 per cent not right, the last two polls in 1983 reflecting discontent with the economic deterioration produced by the war and the prolonged occupation of southern Lebanon rather than outright opposition to the war itself.

The war succeeded in establishing a very important link between the two occupations and Israel's deteriorating economy: thus the peace front could expect support from a large and growing constituency. According to a survey made in 1981 by the Van Leer Jerusalem Foundation, Israeli public opinion was then divided into three segments: 15 per cent racist-extremist, 25 per cent moderate and 60 per cent ambivalent and susceptible to influence by the leadership.[14] After the Lebanon war the ambivalent 60 per cent was less susceptible because it had less confidence in the Government. But this can be elaborated upon: according to Israel Eldad, the Gush Emunim-Tehiya Party ideologue, the core of activists in the Greater Israel lobby amounts to about 5 per cent of the population; this percentage is certainly matched by the radicals who advocate a Palestinian state at the opposite pole; and Peace Now claims that it has the support of about 25 per cent of the population.

Realizing almost immediately that their position had been strengthened by the events of February 1983, Peace Now activists turned their attention to the settlements: in April the group conducted a campaign against the opening of the settlement of 'Bracha' on the outskirts of Nablus, culminating in a demonstration at the inauguration ceremony where 7,000 protesters confronted 1,500 settlers and their supporters. Peace Now and other groups continue to demonstrate against the settlers in Hebron and Nablus, the two West Bank towns which have been targets of Gush Emunim.

Retreat of the Messianic Militarists

The death of a demonstrator and the new balance between the annexationist and peace forces forced the Likud government under the low-key Premier Yitzak Shamir to provide the second Jerusalem march, in February 1984, with both proper protection and extensive radio and television coverage. The 1984 Jerusalem march was significant because it was partly organized by and attended by prominent figures in the Labour Alignment, 28 of its 47 Knesset Members having by that time joined the Party's 'peace forum'. By February 1984 opinion surveys indicated that three out of four Israelis favoured an IDF pull-out from Lebanon. This was because the war and occupation had inflicted hardship on a majority of Israelis — either through military service or through the economic crisis, deepened and magnified by the war.

The removal from centre stage in Israeli political life of the combination of personalities who had launched the IDF into Lebanon enabled the new leadership to pull the forces back to the old international frontier. But before it undertook to do this, the IDF conducted two pull-backs within the country, the first, under American pressure, from West Beirut in October 1982 and the second a year later from the Chouf Mountains. Here the decision to withdraw was taken unilaterally by the IDF command. And when the US asked Israel to postpone its move, Defence Minister Arens replied, 'Sorry, my generals have informed me that our withdrawal cannot be delayed. The wheels are already in motion.' [15]

During the IDF pull-back from West Beirut, Begin and Sharon were immobilized by the furore over the massacre and succumbed to pressure from the military and the US. The second pull-back took place after Sharon and Eitan had been removed from command of the IDF and Begin had resigned. But it took an election and the removal of Begin's colleague Yitzak Shamir from the premiership, and of Moshe Arens from Defence, to compose a Cabinet able to authorize the withdrawal the Israeli public had wanted for 18 months. And, significantly, it was not the war itself, the period of battle from 4 June to 1 September 1982, but the long-drawn-out occupation, particularly of the region south of the Awali River, that decided the question.

The major factor leading to this decision was the casualty toll from the war of attrition waged by the mainly Shite Muslim population of south Lebanon against the Israeli occupation troops. During the official war 345 Israelis were killed; from 2 September 1982 until the decision to withdraw in January 1985 another 270 Israelis had been killed in the multiple daily attacks launched by the resistance. In addition, the Lebanon adventure produced some 5,000 wounded, many of them badly crippled, nearly half being casualties of the war of attrition in the nine months before the Cabinet took its decision. The second factor in the decision was the cost of the occupation, put, by different quarters at $1-2 million a day. The third factor was the general feeling of the Israelis that they had been deceived into backing a massive undertaking that never could have succeeded.

The IDF high command also exerted sustained pressure on the Government for withdrawal from the troop redeployment along the Awali River in the autumn of 1983. The General Staff saw what had been an effective fighting force turned into the demoralized and fearful 'IDF of Lebanon' which hid deep inside its bunkers and shrank from any contact with the local population.

In a letter to the Prime Minister a group of officers and soldiers, including reservists, returning home after a month's service, spelled out the long-term effect the experience in Lebanon could have on the IDF:

> it seems to us that those most affected . . . will be precisely those in the regular army not acquainted with any other IDF than the 'IDF of Lebanon', in which the actions of the army are dictated by circumstances and forces which are not dependent on us, and the result is the impression that we have lost the initiative and control of our fate. The loss of initiative magnifies fear and the feeling of insecurity, and consequently the army closes itself into its bases and camps. [16]

Some units refused orders and others were so demoralized that, after one tour of duty in Lebanon, they could not be sent back. Defections among reservists, ranging from 10 to 60 per cent in various units, placed a heavier burden on those who did serve, many of whom had five or six terms in Lebanon. This increased burden promoted emigration from Israel during both the fighting and the occupation (while emigration took place only after Israel's earlier wars were all over). And many of those who did not opt out by leaving did so through drugs.

The controversy over the nature of the war—was it a war 'of choice' or 'of no alternative' — impaired the IDF's ability to deal with refuseniks and recalcitrants: many officers simply ignored such people, hoping they would go away, as shown by a letter written to a newspaper by a reserve paratrooper, Rami Givoni:

> During the past year I have been called four times to serve . . . and I have disregarded the call. I was called twice to appear before my commanders for a court martial but I did not obey the call. I have not yet been punished for not appearing. [17]

The controversy which began as soon as the IDF set foot in Lebanon also affected the fighting spirit of the troops. Heroics were out: the attitude of the men had changed. Previously individuals strove to stand out in the fighting, promote their 'macho' image and win recognition, but in the IDF of Lebanon the slogan was to be a 'rosh kattan', a 'small head', not a hero. Because of the negative image of this IDF fewer candidates applied for officer training in the Regular Army, particularly from the kibbutzim, and fewer soldiers extended their service beyond the compulsory period. Withdrawal from Lebanon was an act of self-preservation by the IDF, and was seen as such long before the politicians ordered it.

But, as one Israeli commentator put it, this withdrawal was 'a pragmatic switch of strategy, not a decision to turn over a new leaf' [18] —not on the narrow issue of continuing intervention in Lebanese affairs, not on the broad national question of the future of the territories and a settlement with the Palestinians. The Government hoped that the peace front's campaign would lose momentum once the IDF pull-out was underway and that the front would lose the bulk of a single-issue following. The expectation was that Peace Now would subside into dormancy. But this did not happen because, for Peace Now, the war was always a side issue; the real focus of the group's interest and activity has always been the issue of the occupied territories, which is, too, the core of concern for the smaller, more radical groups.

The Emergence of a Political Centre

Some well-informed Israelis believe that a political centre has emerged in Israel, for the first time. The spokesman of the centre is Peace Now which, with the support of about 25 per cent of the population, must be considered the largest peace group in the world in proportion to the population. Since the Lebanon war Peace Now has become the group representing 'normalcy' in a society confused by religio-historical messianism. As the only pro-American peace lobby in the world, Peace Now could have influence with the American Government and appeal for Washington's help in pressing the Israeli Government to moderate its policies.

But because Peace Now has won over the centre it has had to equivocate on its platform. For instance, it was severely criticized by the more radical elements in the peace front for opposing the Lebanon war while insisting that its members do their military service in Lebanon. Peace Now also fails to state clearly how much and what territory it would have Israel leave in order to achieve peace with the Arabs; nor is it ready to say what the political future of the Palestinians should be — confederation with Jordan, an independent state? However, Peace Now can take the credit for the two concrete successes of the peace front since September 1982, the publication in February 1983 of the Kahan Commission report on the Sabra–Chatila massacre and in February 1984 of the report prepared by Assistant Attorney-General Yehudit Karp detailing repression and human rights violations in the occupied territories, a report which was suppressed by the Likud government for 18 months before being released.

Results of the War

The peace front, with all its inconsistencies and weaknesses, is more viable than ever before because the messianic militants, and the messianic militarists, have openly challenged the political nature of the society. Such a challenge was inevitable because the liberal, democratic ideal, adopted by the Zionist Congresses in the twenties, was eroded by creeping militarization during the pre-state period and then, under Ben Gurion, subordinated by the militarists. Although this process had been noted by many Israelis, it was not discussed in polite society. According to peace activist Avraham Burg, before the Lebanon war there were many issues which were 'taboo', not to be discussed, but the war put 'everything on the table', particularly concerning the role of the military. It is interesting that Yoram Peri's book, *Between Battles and Ballots: Israeli Military in Politics*, a rewritten doctoral thesis, came out after the Lebanon war. It is the first major study of the politicization of the Israeli military, a book which pries into the sanctified area of security; it is doubtful if it would have been tolerated before the Lebanon war.

For Israel it is particularly important for everything to be put on the table, for all controversial issues to be under discussion because, as Avraham Burg said, the 'society has still not decided what it is'. At present it is 'part traditional, part modern; part secular, part religious'. And 'as long as it remains undecided there is a vacuum' into which the 'zealots' can move. The zealots 'cannot bear the situation to be without definition' and as a result 'try to overdefine' matters. Such people, he says, have been present in Israel since 1948, and have carefully been developing their ideology and programme since 1967, and after the first Begin government was installed in 1977 they came out into the open, their incubation period completed.

With all the issues on the table and the lines of battle drawn between the two camps, Israelis belonging to the ambivalent 60 per cent have been forced to take sides, causing the society to divide and polarize. And this division has forced both sides to seek support outside the country, in the Diaspora, as earlier peace groups have done. The Labour-affiliated 'International Centre for Peace in the Middle East' (founded in 1982), the Van Leer Jerusalem Institute and the 'New Israel Fund', amongst others, have joined the traditional dovish campaigners of *New Outlook*, the Israel League for Human and Civil Rights, the Israeli Council for Israel-Palestine Peace, the Committee for Just Peace in the Middle East in a new attempt to 'capture' the Diaspora communities. Peace Now has had considerable success in reaching the Diaspora communities: it has several regional offices in the United States where there are local chapters of the 'Friends of Peace Now' — which have also been established in Europe.

One important development has been the creation of independent fund-raising organizations by Israelis and their supporters in the Diaspora who object to United Jewish Appeal-Karen Kayesod funds being used for projects in the occupied territories. One such organization is the New Israel Fund which contributes to civil rights and women's groups, organizations promoting good relations between Palestinians and Israelis, Palestinian boy scouts chapters, neighbourhood development schemes and 'education for peace' projects (publicity).

The Lebanon war enhanced the appeal of the centrist peacemakers. According to Leon Hadar, the correspondent of *The Jerusalem Post* and *Al-Hamishmar* in New York, the attitude of the 'largest Jewish community in the world' is '"don't harm us"'. There are some Jews who are afraid that Israeli policy will endanger their status . . . harm their relations with [non-Jews]. They are unwilling to pay the price of their support in such a way as to cause conflict with their non-Jewish neighbours.' [19] The independent dovish alternative the peace camp offers is a more humane and generally more acceptable Zionism than that promoted by the messianic militants, the World Zionist Organization and the Israeli Government, which have organized their own hard-line lobbies such as 'Americans for a Safe Israel'.

So far this competition for the support of American Jews has had little or no impact on the American Zionist organizations which continue to present a solid front in dealings with Congress and the Administration. Indeed, Congress' double rejection of Presidential bills authorizing the sale of weapons systems to Jordan and Saudi Arabia in the first half of 1986 demonstrated that the official Zionist lobby, the American-Israel Public Affairs Committee, did not even have to use its influence among legislators to ensure that they would take a pro-Israel line. This was particularly true in the case of arms sales to Saudi Arabia when Israel publicly turned off its lobbyists.

Israel, and Zionism, have come full circle; the issues which were on the table during the Zionist Congress during the late twenties and thirties are those being settled today. But now the implications of the outcome are clear: the struggle between the two sides, the two cultures, is for both the body and soul of the state. Will it remain in the modern world as a secular, democratic nation state or will the ultra-nationalistic and messianic fundamentalists force Israel to segregate itself for good in a militaristic ghetto?

Notes

1. New material on the Syrian-Israeli contacts of the fifties has been published in the Hebrew press as a result of the recent opening of Israeli Government records. The monthly *Monitin* carried an article by Yoram Nimrod in February 1984 on the Sharett approach to Syria.

2. Rael Jean Isaac, *Israel Divided: Ideological Politics in the Jewish State* (Baltimore and London: Johns Hopkins, 1976), page 74. This is the standard work on the impact of 1967.

3. Professor Leibowitz is quoted from an article in *The Jewish Chronicle*, 17 September 1982.

4. Isaac, op. cit., page 96.

5. Meron Benvenisti quoted from an article in *The New York Review of Books*, 13 October 1983.

6. Peace Now's information pamphlet was published in October 1982.

7. The Peace Now programme was described by Janet Aviad in a *Jerusalem*

Letter published in January 1980.

8. The abuses of the settlers in the territories were described in a report entitled 'Research on Human Rights in the Occupied Territories, 1979-1983', published by the International Centre for Peace in the Middle East in 1984. See page 51 of the report.

9. The paratrooper's letter was published in *Davar*, 28 June 1982.

10. The letter of the 86 reservists appeared in *The Jerusalem Post*, 9 July 1982. The refusal phenomenon was discussed by Tali Zelinger in *Davar* on 6 May 1983.

11. See Ze'ev Schiff and Ehud Ya'ari, *Israel's Lebanon War* (New York: Simon & Schuster, 1984), pages 54-5, where they point out that Geva opposed the sort of operation that Sharon was planning, long before it was launched, and that his resignation in August came as a result of this opposition and was not a spur of the moment action.

12. David Blundy and Hirsh Goodman broke the mutiny story in *The Sunday Times* almost as soon as it happened: 3 October 1982.

13. Shulamit Hareven's account from which her assessment was taken appeared in *Yedioth Ahronoth*, 14 February 1983.

14. The figures came from Alouph Hareven in an interview at the Van Leer Institute in February 1984.

15. Arens was quoted by Yoram Peri in *The International Herald Tribune*, 20 October 1983.

16. The letter of the soldiers on their experience in Lebanon was quoted by Tamar Meroz in the *Ha'aretz* weekend supplement, 30 March 1984.

17. The letter of the recalcitrant paratrooper, Rami Givoni, was published in *Zu Haderech*, 7 March 1984.

18. The commentator on Labour's switch of strategy was Peretz Kidron in *Middle East International*, 25 January 1985.

19. Leon Hadar in *Al-Hamishmar*, 30 June 1983.

5. The Land Versus the Soul

The Burden of Zionism

The burden that Israel and the Israelis bear is Zionism, which has failed as the ideology of the whole Jewish people. And because of this failure Zionism must reduce its expectations and the scope of its original enterprise — Jewish sovereignty over all of Eretz Yisrael — and tailor its contemporary endeavour to the territory it can manage with the means it possesses. Whatever Zionism attempts to accomplish beyond its limitations must involve both the work of the Palestinian population it rules and military resources it does not have: borrowed labour, borrowed weaponry and borrowed money.

Zionism has not accomplished the in-gathering of a majority of the Jews but only 20-odd per cent of the total. Furthermore there is no prospect — without the spur of another wave of anti-semitism in the West — that there will ever be mass Jewish immigration to Israel. Fewer than 20 per cent of the Soviet Jews who are permitted to leave go to Israel, and among those who do go, there are a significant number who apply for immigration permits for the US and Western Europe. And finally, of the 3.5 million Israelis more than half a million are permanently residing abroad, many holding dual citizenship. According to the 1983 edition of *The Statistical Abstract of Israel* more Israelis than ever are voting with their feet: for the first time the difference between emigration and immigration was a minus figure, 25,000 emigrated while 13,900 immigrated.

Zionism has failed to achieve close Jewish settlement on even the land secured in 1948-9. Indeed, there is a settlement drive in the Galilee district (one of six in the country) where the Palestinian population surpasses the Israeli;[1] furthermore the Negev is being depopulated through emigration to the large towns and cities. In the West Bank 10 per cent of the flats in newly built urban centres are empty, and many Israelis who have bought flats and even moved in, consider the present system of subsidized purchase as an investment opportunity rather than as pioneering. Settlement throughout the Land had failed because the pioneering spirit which drove the first colonists to accept isolation and hardship has waned and been replaced by the consumerist drive for goods and amenable employment. The pattern of employment has reverted to the Diaspora model which was brought by the very first colonists to Palestine: Israelis are the managers and foremen in agricultural and construction work, the Palestinians form the labour force. Thus the Zionist work ethic that the country should be reclaimed by Jewish labour, particularly on the land, and that Jews should be reborn by such labour, has faded. (Indeed, militant nationalists like Israel Eldad decry this state of affairs and would remedy it by expelling the Palestinians.)

Finally, Israel is less and less a spiritual centre for the Jews of the Diaspora because it grows less and less representative of World Jewry in terms of ideology, demography and religion. The Diaspora has become increasingly alienated by the Government's Greater Israel policies and its enthusiastic use of its military power. More than half of Israel's population is Oriental and observant while the Jews of the Diaspora are Ashkenazi and mostly secular, or secularized. And, because of the 1947 Status Quo Agreement between the state-to-be and the Orthodox and Ultra-orthodox rabbis, Israeli life is securely under the control of the conservative Rabbinate, which, encouraged by religious militants, is constantly trying to extend its powers, for instance by closing down the country on the Sabbath and compelling observance in public. One area in which the Orthodox have been trying to gain control for 25 years is in determining a Jew for purposes of immigration to Israel.

To accomplish this the Orthodox have been pressing for an amendment of the Zionist 'Law of Return', enacted in 1950, which stipulates that any person born of a Jewish mother or converted to Judaism is entitled to immigrate. The Orthodox want to add that conversion should be 'according to religious law (Halacha)'. But such an amendment, it is argued, would disrupt the bonds between the state and the Diaspora. According to David Krivine, writing in *The Jerusalem Post*, 'The core of the problem is that Judaism is monolithic in Israel and pluralistic in the Diaspora.' [2] Thus, in Israel, nearly all Jews are formally Orthodox — whether Sephardi or Ashkenazi. But in North America, where the majority of Jews live, only 10 per cent are Orthodox, the rest being Conservative, Reform and Reconstructionist. Immigrants who did not conform to the definition of who is a Jew fixed by the Israeli Rabbinate would, unless they converted, be without personal status in the society, causing problems over marriage, divorce, the legitimacy of children and burial. The recent Ethiopian immigrants faced just this problem — without the proposed amendment. The amendment was put before the Knesset in February 1986 and defeated by 61 votes to 47 (the religious parties plus their Herut–Likud coalition partner), a close enough poll to worry those who did not wish to see a Zionist measure become a religious one, and the global definition of who is a Jew determined by the Orthodox religious authorities in Israel. Israel cannot expect to remain a 'lighthouse to World Jewry' if it first offends then disconnects itself from the greater Diaspora community which both politically and financially underwrites the survival of the state.

Nor could Israel expect consistent support if it emitted confused signals about the state of its psycho-political health. With Zion in its grasp, Zionism realized its goal but alienated half of the Israeli people. And this happened because the Zionist-Israeli leadership forgot about the soul of the people who would live in that Land. But then the Land was the only common objective of the multitude of competing ideological factions that gathered beneath the umbrella of the Zionist Organization, then the Israeli State, until 1967. Thereafter consensual politics gradually gave way to ideological politics, polarizing the society into the two political cultures described in Chapter 1: the first, an extension of Herzl's political Zionism—nationalist, secular, liberal, democratic; the second, an extension of the messianism of the East European ghetto — ultra-nationalist, romantic, dominated by the fundamentalist religious faction which is narrow, chauvinist, authoritarian, segregationist.[3]

Reaffirmation of Militant Zionism

The second political culture declared itself in August 1967 with the creation of the Land of Israel Movement and was strengthened in 1973 by the formal establishment of 'Gush Emunim' ('the Bloc of the Faithful'),[4] as a pressure group within the National Religious Party to prevent it from joining what was considered a concessionist Labour Alignment-led coalition. Until then the NRP had been a moderate party with a dovish wing led by Moshe Unna. Gush Emunim was the extension of a seminary-affiliated youth movement which followed the teachings of the Rabbis Kook. The Gush Emunim attitude was summed up by its spokeswoman as follows:

> For us there was no question but that the liberation of those ancestral territories of the Jewish people was an act of God, the Finger of the Almighty at work. It would be sinful, not politically mistaken, or a security slip, but positively sinful, for us to have permitted the undoing of such a divine act.

Gush Emunim quickly gained the initiative by claiming that the Government's refusal to settle the territories meant that Israel was not fulfilling its ideological commitment to Zionism. The Labour Government was in fact permitting settlement, under military auspices, to lay claim by reasons of 'security', but because of its undertaking to trade territory for peace could not annex the territories or declare its intention to keep them.

When the Labour Alignment was returned to power in 1973, after the October War, the Party was divided between hawks and doves and weakened by internal rivalries. Gush Emunim exploited this situation to gain its settlement objectives, securing Yigal Allon's support for Kiryat Arba, Shimon Peres' for Ofra and Yitzak Rabin's for Kadum-kedumim. From exploitation of political infighting, Gush Emunim moved to physical confrontation with the Government, as described earlier, and this was carried over into the period of Likud rule: in Hebron, once again, where Rabbi Moshe Levinger sent women and children to occupy a Jewish-owned building in the town centre, the sympathetic Begin government allowed them to remain. But outside Nablus a similar probing settlement action was forced to retreat. Gush Emunim was taken as a model by other similarly-minded groups which initiated independent settlement activity, particularly in the Muslim Quarter of the Old City of Jerusalem where 200-odd seminarians have set up 'yeshivot', two of which — 'Ateret Cohanim', 'The Crown of the Priests' and 'Torat Cohanim', 'The Tora Priests' — train priests towards the day they will resume worship in a resurrected Temple beside or, preferably in place of, the Muslim holy places on Mount Moriah.

The messianic militants consider themselves the only real patriots in Israel because they believe that only they strive for the fulfilment of both biblical prophecy and the Zionist dream. For them the Labour and Likud governments have been equally sinful for failing to take immediate and complete possession of the Land. Because they to some extent consider the claim justified and because they want to capitalize on the activities of the militants to promote settlement, the authorities have not dealt forcefully with the illegal activities of the messianics. Wherever they have intruded their presence violence has erupted: in Hebron there has been a continuous stream of incidents, including killings and the arson of the central covered market by Gush Emunim supporters, and in Jerusalem there have been over 100 assaults on the Muslim sanctuary by various groups, including the 'Temple Mount Faithful', the Herut Party's Betar youth movement, Gush Emunim, Kach and delegations led by Knesset Members and a former Chief Rabbi.

The most extreme of the messianics is Kach, the political party founded by the American-born Rabbi Meir Kahane, who was elected to the Knesset in 1984. Kahane began his career with the Jewish Defence League established in the US in 1969; this group carried out bomb attacks against Soviet, PLO and other targets in the US. Kahane has been arrested more than 100 times and served prison sentences in both the US and Israel. He recruits and trains activists in the United States for service in the West Bank. The name of his Party, 'Kach', translates as 'Thus' from the Hebrew; its symbol is a clenched fist. Kach was considered the most extreme of the messianic groups until, in April 1984, the authorities arrested members of an underground network of Israel-born Jewish terrorists in the Gush Emunim settlements of the West Bank, demonstrating that the Kach methodology had been adopted by the mainstream in the ideological settler movement. Messianic ideology and ultra-nationalism propel the militants into violence. And they believe that it is the duty of Jews to break the laws of Israel if the higher interests, as defined by them, of the 'Jewish people' are at stake.

Kahane calls for the expulsion of the 700,000 Palestinians who are Israeli citizens as well as the 1.3 million who live in the territories. He believes that Israel must become an all-Jewish theocracy where the Tora is the law:

> I'm taking on people steeped in Western concepts who tell themselves that Judaism is really Thomas Jefferson or Burke or Rousseau when it's really nothing of the sort . . . Judaism was always an exclusive group and it doesn't integrate with other people. I'm a Jew, not a democrat.[5]

He castigates the Israeli authorities for failing to 'get rid' of the Palestinians in 1967 when 'the Lord gave us the opportunity to do so'.

After the Rabbi's election to the Knesset in July 1984, Dani Rubinstein commented on the phenomenon of Kahanism:

> Maybe Kahane is right and he is just beginning his political ascent. There is no question about it that Kahane is the true representative of political desires no longer hidden among large portions of the Israeli Jewish society. Actually Kahane says openly what Yuval Ne'eman [Minister of Science under the Likud] and his friends [of the Tehiya Party] mutter quietly and what [Rabbi Chaim] Drukman and his Morasha Party [a militant seccessionist faction of the NRP] think loudly. Moreover: Among the hundreds and thousands who vote for and support the Likud [particularly the lower middle and working classes of Orientals] there is deep sympathy 'for Rabbi Kahane'. One often hears people say that 'we must finish [the Palestinians] off', talk about 'trucks' (for deportation), etc. We hear this [sort of talk] every day on the street corner, in buses and markets . . . [and] in 'civilized' salons in wealthy suburbs . . . in the kibbutzim, among students. It is obvious that over the past few years Kahane's views have been legitimized . . . Actually Kahanism is a phenomenon which had to grow in the context of the binational reality, the background of terroristic activity and the semi-messianic and nationalistic atmosphere.[6]

Kahanism has had a striking impact on both the territories and Israel proper: everywhere the level of violence has been rising. In the territories it is a fact of daily life. Military repression has increased, with shootings of demonstrators, administrative detention of political activists in a new prison near Nablus, restriction orders confining others to their homes or towns. More than 3,000 Palestinians from the territories are in Israeli prisons, the majority for security offences, and it is estimated that one-sixth of the total population of the territories have since 1967 passed through the hands of the security authorities. In April 1984 two Palestinians who had hijacked an Israeli bus were beaten to death by security officials immediately after the Army had stormed the bus and freed the passengers. The then Defence Minister Moshe Arens declared on television soon after the incident: 'Whoever plans terrorist acts in Israel must know he won't get out alive.' The words were later embroidered with clarifications saying that he had not meant that 'terrorists' captured alive would be executed on the spot, but Arens' message came across loud and clear.

It was a message which was unacceptable to many influential Israelis, in particular the Attorney-General Yitzak Zamir, who kept open his file on the case and pressed the police to continue with their investigations. Then in May 1986 Zamir made public his demand that Avraham Shalom, head of the General Security Services (Shin Beth), should resign. Zamir said he had evidence that Shalom had ordered that the two Palestinians should be clubbed to death and later covered up his agency's role in the affair to the extent of lying to three commissions of inquiry. Once the story broke the press disclosed that Shalom had received 'approval' for Shin Beth's actions from none other than the then Prime Minister, Yitzak Shamir.[7] Both the serving Premier, Peres, and the Cabinet resisted Zamir's demand for a full public policy inquiry and, on 1 June, at the height of the controversy, Zamir's resignation, which had been tendered in February, was accepted by the Cabinet and a replacement appointed to take over his post on 4 June.

According to *The Times*'s Jerusalem correspondent, Christopher Walker, 'Gun law rules in the wild West Bank': Israel imposes laws on the use but not the carrying of guns by civilians; any settler over the age of 16 may receive from the IDF an army-issue weapon for self-defence; such guns are carried at political demonstrations; there are a great many licensed hand guns distributed among the civilian population throughout Israel — as a group of Palestinian guerrillas discovered to their cost when they were gunned down while carrying out a grenade attack in central Jerusalem in 1984. Indeed the targets displayed in shops specializing in hand guns are not the usual bullseye but the silhouette of a man. There is also a flourishing black market in stolen IDF grenades, mortars, rifles, even mines. Some IDF issue has also been used by Palestinian guerrillas in attacks inside Israel. [8]

The logical consequence of Kahanism and gun law was the Jewish underground and terrorist network. These settlers, frustrated over what they saw as the Government's inability to prevent all Palestinian resistance, particularly incidents of stone-throwing, and convinced that attacks on Palestinians would encourage them to leave, 'took *the law* into their own hands [my italics]', to use the words applied to them by their supporters. These militants simply did in an organized way what others had been doing for several years on an *ad hoc* basis, with the Government looking the other way or suppressing Palestinian complaints against the settlers. As Deputy Attorney-General Yehudit Karp said in her report: 'Jewish settlers had been given to understand at some high level that they were under no obligation to cooperate with the police.' [9]

It was only because members of the main underground were arrested in April after an aborted attempt to place bombs on four West Bank buses that such operations were publicly connected with Gush Emunim. Before then attacks on Palestinian targets were believed to have been carried out by lunatic fringe elements operating independently. One such group called itself 'Terror Against Terror'; nine of its members were arrested in December 1983 after the unveiling of another conspiracy to blow up the Dome of the Rock in the sanctuary on Mount Moriah. Among the members of the settlers' network were two Army officers employed in the West Bank Military Government who knew of the plan to attack the three Palestinian mayors in 1980 and connived in its execution. Other members were respected leaders of the Gush Emunim movement, men whose past record, in the words of a defender, showed them to be 'decent and honourable people' who were merely trying to protect themselves in their 'own' land. [10] Widespread public support for the underground defendants, and the privileged treatment accorded to them by the authorities during their incarceration and trial, demonstrated that their actions were approved, or excused, by at least one-third of the Israeli population. Pressure for their release built up in May 1985 after a prisoner exchange between a Damascus-based dissident Palestinian group and Israel, which involved the release in the territories of some 700 Palestinian security prisoners. In 1986 President Herzog granted several of the minor underground members early release.

Militarization of the Mind

The Israelis have only themselves, and their leaders, to blame for this rallying of a substantial proportion of the population behind the Jewish underground, because those who have formed public opinion, since before the founding of the state, have propagated the idea that the Arab hostility to Israel was implacable and that Israel had to fight in order to exist. Such proportions ensured public acceptance of near-perpetual reserve military service and enabled the politico-military establishment to sustain the disproportionately large army required for the full realization of the Zionists' territorial objective rather than merely defending the state within its 1948-9 borders.

The distortion of the totality of Israeli life, of the Israeli psyche, the country's politics, social system and external relations flowed from that fateful 1954 decision of the Ben Gurion government—with the enthusiastic backing of Moshe Dayan and the military establishment — to refuse the American offer of frontier guarantees. Once that decision had been taken the public mind had to be prepared for the unending struggle ahead by a campaign to demonize the enemy. Israel's expert on Arab attitudes to Israel, Professor Yehoshafat Harkabi provided, in his numerous books and journalistic writings, the raw material for the programme introduced in the media, schools and the IDF, the State's most powerful institution. This campaign influenced or formed the opinions of at least the 60 per cent of the population born since the establishment of the state, and more than half of this 60 per cent is of Oriental origin. These Israelis are therefore moved by the struggle which has involved them for the whole of their lives rather than the wider concerns of older Zionists — Nazism and anti-semitism, the defence of human rights and democratic values. Israeli attention first focused on the Arabs in neighbouring states who were expected to avenge their Palestinian brothers and reclaim Arab land, then after 1967 on the Palestinians themselves, with whom there was the distorted relationship produced by occupation and resistance.

After the educational structure, the IDF has played a key role in moulding public opinion — through its own education service, its large-scale publishing activities, the Army radio and the Military Rabbinate Brigade which is the representative of the religious establishment in the armed forces. The military rabbinate has had particular influence over young conscript soldiers. It equates the contemporary struggle between Israel and the Palestinians with the ancient conflict between the Jews and the Amalek (whom God permitted the Jews to destroy), and issues opinions saying that it is a soldier's duty to kill or expel anyone who opposes Israel. During the Lebanon fighting, which the rabbinate designated as a 'divinely inspired war' ('milhemet mitzva') a daily reading was recommended of Psalm 83, calling for the destruction by fire and tempest of the enemies of Israel. The military rabbinate also issued a map which laid claim to large areas of southern Lebanon as the inheritance of modern Israel bequeathed by one of the original twelve tribes of Israel, the Tribe of Asher, which once possessed the territory between the Chouf Mountains and Sidon. The Sephardi Chief Rabbi also ruled that wounded Jewish soldiers should not be given non-Jewish blood unless their lives were endangered, and even then it was better not to begin such a practice as 'it takes Jewish blood to cure Jews.'[11]

It was no accident that an apparently mild-mannered Israeli soldier encamped in the suburbs of Beirut in 1982 told the correspondent of *The Times*, 'Listen . . . I know you are tape-recording this but personally I would like to see them all dead. I would like to see all the Palestinians dead because they are a sickness wherever they go.'[12] A 'sickness'. Or else, 'terrorists'. When referring to Palestinians, Israelis automatically employ the word 'terrorists', some specifically for the PLO and its fighters, but many for the whole people. This lack of differentiation between guerrillas and civilians goes right back to the pre-state struggle when the Haganah took up the practice of 'retaliating' for Palestinian raids against armed settlements by making counter-raids against villages, armed or unarmed. This policy was refined in the fifties by Ben Gurion, becoming Israel's 'reprisal doctrine' — which, in fact, had nothing to do with reprisals, but involved offensive actions along the frontiers to heighten tension and provide the IDF with military opportunities. The planting of the word 'terrorist' in the minds of many Israelis caused them to dehumanize the entire Palestinian people, and anyone who offers them sanctuary, like the Lebanese, who in 1982, paid a high price for the Palestinian presence in Lebanon. And because of this designation, the Israelis suspect every Palestinian political initiative, whether coming from the PLO or independents, considering anything coming from the Palestinians as being designed to harm Israel. Those Israelis who have seen beyond the propaganda to the substance of the conflict and are prepared to make concessions for peace, are considered by the others as 'traitors' or naive 'beautiful souls'.

From Verbal Violence to Political Violence

During the fighting in Lebanon, supporters of the war calling themselves the 'national camp', that is the patriotic camp, conducted a telephone campaign of abuse against journalists, Knesset members and other personalities who had voiced their opposition. Those not in the national camp were designated by such epithets as 'cosmopolitans' and 'self-hating intellectuals'. Victor Shem-Tov, the Secretary-General of the Mapam Party, was repeatedly threatened: 'Mr Shem-Tov, you are a traitor! Your days are numbered. You shall be shot in the head.' He replied in a letter to the press 'directed at the true assassin. He is not one of those who call me to curse and threaten . . . My real assassin is a collective . . . The best speakers in the Knesset take part in my assassination, as well as writers belonging to a certain ideological school' — which promotes verbal and physical violence.[13] Another Member of the Knesset who was threatened[14] took up the matter with the Deputy Speaker of the Knesset, a member of Herut, who explained that such threats were the only way the 'small man' could express his anger over criticism he believed was 'insulting' to the Prime Minister and the nation.

During the crisis over the formation of the commission of inquiry on the massacre in October 1982, a new paper called the *Weekly Diary* appeared in which 'the Left' was attacked for 'undermining national morale . . . sabotaging national interests . . . blood libel directed at public figures . . . giving political weapons to the enemies of the state'. With the exception of the 'blood libel' charge, all these formulations have been used to great advantage by the many populist regimes the world has experienced. To these the Begin and Sharon enthusiasts added their own verbal tactic, used to great effect against the 1983 Peace Now demonstration in Jerusalem. This consists of simply chanting the name of the preferred hero for fifteen to twenty minutes either in demonstration of support for that hero during his rally or against the opposition to obstruct its meeting. The 'Begin, Begin' chant was used to disrupt a protest meeting against the Sabra–Chatila massacre on the second day of Rosh Hashana outside Jerusalem's Grand Synagogue where Begin was attending a service.[15] Then, according to an eyewitness, the protesters were 'violently attacked by [Begin's] supporters, who lunged into them with fists flying'. It was what the witness called, 'another episode in the wars of the Jews'. And the most shocking aspect of the incident was that no one 'tried to break up the melee', including the Prime Minister who 'only had to say a few words...and the fighting would have stopped'.[16]

The war provided an occcasion for the zealots and their supporters, frustrated to the point of hysteria, to attack their opponents, particularly the anti-war demonstrators whom they abused and assaulted throughout the summer, and without police intervention since the attitude of the police mirrored that of Begin. It was surprising that the first fatality fell only in February 1983.

Verbal violence even dominated the deliberations of the 30th Zionist Congress meeting in Jerusalem in December 1982, causing *The Jerusalem Post* to charge that 'the Congress can represent Zionism only by stretching it to the breaking point'.[17]

The Lebanon war failed first and foremost to put an end to Palestinian violence against Israelis in the occupied territories. Instead this violence increased and crossed the Green Line into Israel when Palestinian citizens of the state joined in the murderous attacks. And an entirely new phenomenon emerged: attacks which are, in the words of former IDF governor of the West Bank and current Knesset Member (Yahad Party), Binyamin Ben-Eliezer, 'spontaneous and unlinked to any terrorist organization'. Sixty-two per cent of the attacks in the territories are of this spontaneous variety. The territories are heading for 'a rebellion or mass civil disobedience' campaign and that 'within three to five years' Israel would 'have a full-scale revolt' on its hands.[18] It may come sooner. By March 1986 the average number of bombings a month had reached 20. In 1985 violent acts, involving guns, explosives and fire bombs, in the West Bank alone averaged more than three a day. Less serious incidents, characterized as 'violations of public order', averaged more than six a day. Some 1,224 'security violations' of the serious type were on the police books in 1985, 18 per cent more than in 1984.[19]

It was not only political violence that made its way across the Green Line from the territories into Israel. There has been an upsurge of racial discrimination against Palestinians applying for such things as taxi licences and seeking housing in Jewish neighbourhoods. In Nazareth[20] controversy over the so-called 'Arab invasion' of the new Jewish development town situated on hills above the old Arab town caused local members of the national camp to organize a committee called 'Mena', 'Prevention', to stop Palestinians, who are Israeli citizens, from moving into the upper town. The Labour-affiliated mayor of the upper town opposes the influx of Palestinians: 'We are a Jewish town of 25,000 in close proximity to 110,000 Arabs. We came to live next to each other but not with one another.' The crisis in Nazareth led several rabbis to issue opinions that Jews and non-Jews should not live in the same buildings or even the same neighbourhoods; though non-Jews should not be permitted to move into Jewish areas, the door was kept open for Jews to settle in non-Jewish areas, such as Hebron and Nablus.

The police increasingly use force when making arrests for common offences. 'It's dangerous to dispute a traffic ticket these days,' remarked one Israeli. Demonstrating El Al workers, on strike for higher pay, were dispersed by flailing police clubs, and police action to demolish an illegal addition to a house in Tel Aviv resulted in the death of an Oriental Jew. Journalist Yael Cohen commented on the second incident: 'It seems to me that the vicious circle of violence that had its beginning in the Casba of Hebron and in the stifling alleyways of the refugee camps in the West Bank has come full circle in Tel Aviv.' Because this connection concerning the rising level of violence in both places has been made in the minds of most Israelis, the Likud government in its last six months in office, was compelled to curb its own worst abuses of power, particularly to arrest the settler underground which had been infiltrated by the internal security forces two years before the exposure.

The arrest of the settler underground represented a small but significant retreat of Israeli society from the fantasies of the messianic militarists and signalled a disengagement of the Likud establishment from the more militant factions of the Gush Emunim movement. The underground apparently had the same relationship with the Likud as did the Revisionists to the Labour Zionists—the Irgun and Stern Gang to the Haganah—during the pre-state struggle. The underground engaged in activites desired by the leadership but not the society as a whole, although, according to Israel Shahak, there is, and always has been, 'some regard for [the zealots] among the majority of Israeli Jews, who both admire and fear these fanatics.'[21] This toleration enabled the underground core to expand from its Kiryat Arba base into other West Bank, Golan and Gaza settlements.

The fantasy that Sharon and Eitan entertained concerning the possibility of a mass flight of Palestinians from southern Lebanon and the Beirut area to Jordan, had also taken root in the minds of those settlers who joined the underground — regarding what force could accomplish in the territories. Professor Harkabi's explanation for the involvement of 'serious people with a solid public standing' in the underground was

> that they are rational people whose chief motivation stems from their awareness that annexation of the West Bank together with its Arab population would be disastrous and tantamount to national suicide — unless that population were thinned out and made to flee by means of terrorism . . . [It is] the logical, rational conclusion of the policy that aims at annexation. Such terrorism is neither a 'punishment' nor a deterrent; it is a political instrument. [22]

The exposure of the underground intensified an existing rift in the settlement movement and the messianic camp between those who favoured such activity — like former Science Minister Yuval Ne'eman of the Tehiya Party, displaced Yamit Rabbi Yisrael Ariel, and Rabbi Moshe Levinger of Kiryat Arba — and more moderate elements who saw the underground as a threat to the entire settlement movement. Rival factions held meetings to 'condemn the underground' or 'condemn the condemners'.

The 1984 Election Campaign [23]

The disarray in the national camp, rivalries within the Likud Cabinet and the rapid deterioration of the economy eroded the ruling party's position: opinion polls showed a decisive shift to Labour. A Knesset election was set for the end of July after the Government lost a vote of confidence due to the defection of the small Oriental Tami Party. The campaign was characterized by its lack of momentum and the low-key approach of both the major parties — in contrast to the riveting noisy and violent campaigns run by the Likud in 1977 and 1981. The Party realized that the political atmosphere in the country would not be conducive to its traditional 'hot' style of campaigning and was even compelled to withdraw its 'national camp' slogan because of its crude ultra-nationalist connotation.

Labour operated under the slogan, 'the only hope', which, for many Israelis, it indeed was. But Labour was considered by the peace front a 'hope' only in comparison with the Likud. In the ten years following the 1967 war Labour was never a prisoner of the Land of Israel Movement — which its Allon Plan pre-empted — but a willing accomplice, though the Party would progress at what it considered an appropriate speed under appropriate — security — cover. Therefore its dovish aspect did not fool the peace front.

During the election campaign Labour tried to be all things to all voters: it sought to attract the 25 per cent of the electorate sympathetic to Peace Now as well as the more hawkish elements among the ambivalent voters and the floaters. Thus Labour leader Peres appointed as his campaign manager Knesset Member Mordechai Gur, a middle-of-the-road figure known for his opposition to the Lebanon war, to secure the moderates, and designated as his adviser for publicity and information, a key post, the Alignment's most notable dove, Yossi Sarid, whose elevation was intended to reassure the more dovish factions of the Peace Now lobby. Meanwhile Peres himself repeatedly declared that a Labour-led government would not dismantle a single settlement.

Shifra Blass, the American-born spokeswoman of the Settlers' Council, confirmed Labour's credentials in a statement during the campaign: 'There are quite a few of us who believe that . . . Labour's traditional warm regard for pioneering settlement will override all other considerations. In this respect it is true that the Likud . . . has never had the strong emotions for settlement and for the land that Labour has.' [24]

Labour's policy platform was based on the three hard-line principles: no negotiations with the PLO, no Palestinian state between Jordan and Israel, no dismantling of existing settlements — the last principle amounting to a reversal of its original policy of confining settlement to areas designated in the Allon Plan, and an affirmation of the right of Israelis to settle everywhere in the territories.

This clear line notwithstanding, the Labour Alignment adopted two conflicting declaratory policies during the campaign. The left-wing Mapam Party spoke to the conciliators and the peace front of a freeze on settlements, the Reagan Plan instead of Camp David as a basis for negotiations, and flexibility on West Bank autonomy. Meanwhile the right wing promoted Camp David with no settlement freeze because continued settlement would keep up the pressure on the Arabs to negotiate. This duality led Labour to try to keep a low profile on the question of the peace process — the most important problem Israel faces.

In spite of Likud Premier Yitzak Shamir's stirring proclamation at the beginning of the campaign that his party would 'tell every voter that it is in his hands to decide the fate of the Land of Israel', the Likud also allowed the issue to slip into the background. It did this because the Government's massive financial outlay on the settlements had alienated a significant proportion of the Likud's lower income constituency which had suffered from the reduction in social and educational programmes.

This simultaneous withdrawal from the area of confrontation over the peace process amounted to active collusion by the two parties to avoid Israel's most pressing, and explosive, problem. The Lebanon war was also relegated to the background. The major campaign issue was the economic mess, which was a direct result of the Likud's fantastic settlement and military policies.

The Result of the 1984 Election

In the immediate aftermath of the Sabra–Chatila massacre it was estimated that the society was divided into three parts: one-third for Begin and Sharon, one-third against them and one-third undecided. By election time, 22 months later, the undecided had split into two near-equal parts and joined the 'for' and 'against' camps. It had been predicted by many informed observers of the Israeli scene that a substantial proportion of the Likud's disillusioned Oriental supporters would abstain, but when the time came they voted for the Likud — without enthusiasm. And the same was true for Labour: many old supporters took the Party's slogan to heart and backed the 'only hope' because they longed to keep the Likud out of power.

This negativism showed in the result: both major parties lost, the Likud 7 seats and Labour 3. The parties which gained were those closest to the poles: the ultra-nationalist-messianic camp — Tehiya, Shas, Agudat Yisrael, Tami, Morasha and Kach — gained 5 seats; and the independent and Labour-aligned doves — Shinui, the Citizens' Rights Movement and the Progressive List for Peace — also gained 5. The doves' unofficial ally the pro-Moscow Democratic Front for Peace and Equality ('Hadash') sustained its representation at 4 seats. Thus, the polar totals were 15 for the ultra-nationalist-messianic camp and 12 for the peace front in comparison with 10 and 7 in 1981. Towards the centre the fractured National Religious Party lost 2 seats and the Ometz splinter of the Telem Party (of the late Moshe Dayan) lost one seat while the hawkish-dovish Yahad Party of former Defence Minister, Ezer Weizman, formed to contest the election, took 3 seats. These changes did not, however, signify a shift in the strength of the two major blocs, but instead involved a realignment of the fringe elements within them. The Labour Alignment won 44 seats on its own and its pledged allies Shinui (3 seats) and the Citizens' Rights Movement (3 seats) and Ometz (one seat) gave the Alignment another 7, making a total of 51, to which could be added another 6 seats from the Progressive List for Peace and Hadash. These two parties could not be taken on as formal allies because of their joint Arab–Jewish membership and their platforms, considered by the majority of Israelis as anti-Zionist.

The Likud secured 41 seats on its own and could count on the backing of Tehiya (5 seats), Shas (4 seats), Agudat Yisrael (2 seats), Morasha (2 seats) and Tami (one seat), if it were asked to form a coalition, on the basis of 55 seats, plus one from the extremist Kach.

On the basis of the numerical strengths of the blocs and their allies, Labour commanded a possible 57 seats and the Likud 56. Israel had, as most political commentators put it, voted itself into a political deadlock. And the deadlock could not be broken by addition of the remaining two parties to the equation. And both staunchly refused to link themselves with either bloc until they saw which was asked to form a government. But if the Likud-leaning NRP had allied itself with that bloc and the Likud-rejecting Yahad had chosen the Labour Alignment there would have been absolute parity.

The result defied opinion polls and confounded the political pundits, particularly because the Oriental voters were not swayed in their support of the Likud by the economic distress that party's policies had caused them. The result confirmed the division of Israel into the two socio-political cultures, separated by ideology, education and economic and social status. Also it was clear that ideology had become a key factor because the two blocs lost votes not to each other but to their respective ideological fringe allies. The overall picture was of stable polarization.

If the election demonstrated the loyalty of the Likud's following, it showed that the loyalty of Labour supporters was shaky and conditional. And it was so because the leadership of the Alignment had refused to take a clear policy line on the future of the territories. Although 28 members of the parliamentary Labour Alignment had joined its peace forum, peace front voters did not see this reflected in the Alignment's election platform, which had instead made it clear that the Party was itself deeply divided on the peace issue. This also explains the net increase of 114,000 votes made by the dovish lists — including 14,000 won by Lova Eliav, an independent candidate who missed a seat by 2,500 votes.

Israeli society reacted to the deadlock by immediately calling for the formation, for the second time in the state's history, of a national unity government. Three days after the 23 July poll, 81 per cent of those responding to a telephone survey said they supported a national unity government, 16 per cent were opposed and the rest had no opinion.[25] The impulsion to form such a government came mainly from the Likud rather than Labour, which, typically, was divided between those in favour and those opposed, particularly the Mapam portion of the Alignment which had the power to withdraw its six seats. But the Likud knew from the outset that it could not be the leading partner in a national unity government because the Labour Alignment could not expect its Mapam colleagues or its dovish allies to join a government under the Likud. In the event, the doves refused to join the Labour-led coalition with the Likud which was constituted in such a way as to give Labour the opportunity to lead during the first half of the Government's four-year term and the Likud during the second half, as long as Yitzak Shamir would be appointed Prime Minister. In addition, this arrangement cost Labour the allegiance of its chief dove Yossi Sarid who deserted to the Citizens' Rights Movement. Thus the defection of Mapam cost the Party 6 seats and effectively cancelled the Alignment, defection of its ally the CRM, 4 seats, and loss of its member, Yossi Sarid, one seat—a total of 11.

Labour spent six arduous weeks forming a national unity government in which it became the weaker component, with 37 seats of its own plus 3 of Shinui and one of Ometz; the Likud having 41 seats of its own, plus 4 from Shas, 2 from Agudat Yisrael and 2 from Morasha. And Yahad and the NRP, opportunists to the core, were more than ready to join the uncertain coalition.

In the push and pull of Cabinet formation three sops were thrown to the peace front: there would be no formal annexation of the territories during the government's term of office, existing settlements would not be expanded by new housing and of the 28 settlements approved by the outgoing government but still on paper, only six located in the areas designated in the Allon Plan, would be founded in the first year. The national unity formula was hailed only by politicians so avid for office that they were prepared to accept a total political freeze and by voters who wished to see the socio-territorial status quo preserved.

Soon after taking over as Prime Minister, Peres characterized the national

111

unity coalition as a government of 'national disagreement'. This has been proved abundantly true. The sole issue on which Labour and Likud could agree was on the need for the imposition of stringent government spending cuts and of wage ceilings to force down inflation. Here the government was successful. It reduced inflation from its spectacular 1,000–800 per cent per annum in 1984 to about 16 per cent by mid-1986. This achievement was helped by the dramatic fall in oil prices in late 1985 and early 1986, which the Government passed on to the consumer. And because of this success in bringing down inflation there developed a tug-of-war between Peres and his Likud (Liberal Party) Finance Minister, Yitzak Moda'i, which resulted in a Cabinet crisis and Government reshuffle in April, just when the public had begun to feel the effects of the reduced inflation.

In other areas of economic policy the Peres government met with failure: crises broke out in the ministries of health, education and social services because of the lack of funds for their programmes. There was a crisis in the IDF over the recruitment of career soldiers because their salaries had been frozen at such low levels. A large number of public and private firms were forced to close down because of indebtedness (some twelve major public companies owe to Israeli banks more than $2,000 million, and a similar amount to foreign investors[26]).

In the foreign policy sphere Peres and his Foreign Minister Shamir made contradictory policy proclamations. There were constant Cabinet crises on every major issue discussed by it. The most serious was a running battle over the adoption by the Knesset of a bill outlawing racism, which the religious parties opposed because certain Jewish religious practices might, under such a law, be defined as racist incitement, particularly those forbidding Jews from dealing with or living next to non-Jews.

During the life of his government Peres was repeatedly accused of trying to exploit the Cabinet crises in order to bring down the national unity government and either force the President to ask Peres to try to form a narrowly based government or precipitate an election in which Labour might secure a large enough share of the vote to put together a more manageable coalition. But at the climax of every crisis the religious parties, determined that the rotation agreement should survive and Peres hand over to Shamir, intervened and mediated a compromise. This mediating role increased the influence of the religious parties over the two major parties to the extent that the Knesset could not enact legislation which the religious parties did not like.

Realignment

Although there is a residual loyalty to the old Zionist Labour and Revisionist structures, other, informal alignments with new ideological formations have appeared between and within the two blocs. This realignment has produced an area of agreement, and even a negotiating position, between Likud moderates and Labour Hawks, and another between the concessionist wing of Labour and the moderates of the peace front. The outer edges of this revised political map are occupied by the messianic-ultra-nationalist factions and the anti-Zionist, pro-Palestinian state factions, each side with 10-12 per cent of the vote. Next to the ultras is a truncated Herut 'Iron Wall' faction and towards the centre a 'federalist' faction which promotes an Israeli-Jordanian condominium in the West Bank and Gaza, or what is called 'shared rule' (amounting to a reworked version of Begin's autonomy scheme for the Palestinians). [27] The federalists share with the rest of the Land of Israel camp the 'not one inch' approach to the disposition of the territories, that is no return of land for peace — which means this approach is unacceptable to the Arabs. But the federalists would neither expel the Palestinians nor institute permanent Israeli military rule over them; under the scheme the Palestinians would be expected to retain Jordanian nationality and find political expression in Jordan while the Israelis would continue to settle and live in the territories and be subject to Israeli law; sovereignty would be shared. On the Labour side at the centre is the 'Jordanian option' faction which advocates the return to Jordan of some territory after Israel has made its security arrangements: essentially involving Israel retaining control over the areas specified in the Allon Plan as well as East Jerusalem, Gaza and the Golan. Then, between the centre-Labour position and the Palestinian state faction is the 'Reagan Plan' faction, favouring the granting of self-determination to the Palestinians on condition that the choice would be predetermined and involve the creation of a state in the territories which would be closely associated with Jordan.

The new political map is outlined in Table 5.1. (See also Appendix.) It is immediately apparent that the formalization of such a realignment would, on the territorial question, reproduce at a new place on the political map, the present division between those Israelis who are prepared to trade territory for peace and those who are not — the 'not one inch' camp. The 'not one inch' camp would have 60 per cent of popular support against the concessionist camp's 40 per cent. Thus this map better reflects the political positions on the territorial/peace issue than one simply showing the two cultures and formal political blocks.

It is clear that Israel, on its own, is not prepared, for the foreseeable future, to offer the Palestinians and the Arabs the minimum they would be ready to accept in exchange for full peace with Israel. But on the more optimistic side, the Palestinian State, Reagan Plan and Federalist factions, with 60 per cent of public support, oppose extreme measures against the Palestinians in the territories and form an important majority favouring Israel's continuation as a democracy. However, as long as the fate of the territories remains undecided, both formally and practically, Israel can expect increasing pressure and more violence from the angry and frustrated messianic/ultra-nationalist elements.

But the struggle for the soul of Israel is not only, or even primarily, between Israelis who would keep the occupied territories and those who would give them up; the true struggle is between religious and secular, between Jewish fundamentalism and the modern world.

Table 5.1

	Small Israel Camp Labour		Greater Israel Camp Likud	
Palestinian State Faction	Reagan Plan Faction	Federalist Faction	Iron Wall Faction	Messianic/ Ultra- nationalist Faction
		(Political Parties)		
Hadash PLP*	CRM† Peace Now Labour Peace Forum	Moderate Likud: La'am & Liberals NRP Yahad Ometz	Herut	Tehiya Shas Kach Morasha Agudat Yisrael
		(Percentage of the Vote)		
10%	30%	30%	18%	12%
	First Culture New Political Centre		Second Culture	

*Progressive List for Peace
†Citizens' Rights Movement

Kulturkampf

The society is under growing pressure from the Orthodox religious establishment to conform to observant norms. This has been accompanied by the self-segregation of the Orthodox and Ultra-orthodox in neighbourhood ghettoes or restricted townships like the Emanuel settlement in the West Bank. Furthermore, as it has been pointed out, the Oriental community has been making a cultural and social reassessment, rejecting the Western, modern Ashkenazi style of life and realigning themselves with the Orthodox religious community which emphasizes social tradition, limitations on the mixing of men and women, strict observance of the Sabbath and fasting and high holy days. This new push-and-pull situation is potentially more explosive than the issue of the territories because it involves internal rather than external relations, of Jews with Jews rather than Israelis with Palestinians.

The confrontation between the two cultures has arisen because each would impose its will on the other: the liberal democrats say that the Israelis must be free to pursue the kind of life each person chooses; the religious and social conservatives say that, as a Jewish state, Israel and its citizens must conform to traditional Jewish practice and religious observance, at least publicly. The former would impose the universalist/humanistic mould of the contemporary world while the latter would reintroduce the narrow segregationist theocratic system of the past, the East European ghetto. There is no way to bridge such a gap between these mutually exclusive approaches to the Israeli polity and the nature of the society. The frustration of the Orthodox has always led to violence, ever since they began to establish themselves in numbers in Palestine in the twenties, but now they have a mass following, and since 1982-3 a violent backlash has developed among those who are unprepared to accept the strictures the religious reactionaries would impose.

Because the ultra-nationalists and messianics insist that Israel retain all the Land, and would force the society to change in order to make this possible, the outcome for the struggle of the soul of Israel will be determined, to a great extent, on the struggle for the Land. There are only two possibilities: Israel keeps all of the Land or Israel gives up a part of it. The Land has, and has had, its price — financial, social, political, moral. If Israel digests the territories occupied in 1967, then it will be necessary to remain a fortress state relying on its own and borrowed military might to protect its occupation and ensure its survival. Because Israel would have to suppress its 40 per cent Palestinian minority and deny it rights in order to maintain the state's Jewish character, Greater Israel would have to become less democratic and more authoritarian (or else expel the bulk of the Palestinians). And because Greater Israel would have to rely for political support on the religious establishment and the conservative Oriental elements, its authoritarianism would be increasingly influenced by the theocrats who seek to transform the society from secularism to religious orthodoxy.

The Material Cost of Keeping the Land

The financial cost of absorbing the territories is far beyond Israel's means, as its experience under Likud rule demonstrated. Israel would be able to afford Labour's policy of creeping annexation but not Begin's massive settlement programme. When Begin came to power in 1977 there were seven civilian settlements in the West Bank; he immediately proposed the construction of 15. This signalled a fundamental change in settlement policy: the Likud authorized the building of tens of permanent rural and urban communities on both state-controlled public land and newly requisitioned land in and around urban concentrations of the Palestinian population. Between 1977 and 1981 a further 17 new settlements were created and existing settlements expanded, the distinction between paramilitary security settlements and civilian ones disappearing altogether. In 1977 there were a total of 5,023 Jewish settlers — both military and civilian — in the West Bank; in 1981, 16,119 settlers; in 1982, an estimated 22,000; in 1984, about 27,000; in January 1985, 42,500; and in January 1986, 52,000. Between 1977 and 1979 the annual allocation for such development was $100 million; in 1981, $160 million; and for 1983-4 at least $470 million, not including an additional $80-100 million a year in Government subsidies to the settlers. [28]

The major settlement drive was outlined in the 'Master Plan for the Development and Settlement of Judea and Samaria' prepared in 1983 by the Settlement Department of the World Zionist Organization. This has the aim of placing one million settlers in the area over a 15–20-year period, not new immigrants but Israelis who normally live across the Green Line. According to a report in the Israeli press,

> An interim goal of the plan is to establish 57 additional communities by mid-1986, bringing the total to 165, at which time . . . 25,000 Jewish families or 125,000 individuals will be living there . . . In the first ten years of implementation of the plan [total] national expenditure . . . will amount to $300 million a year. There is talk of expenditures which will amount in the coming decade to $3 billion; and that is not all, since during that period, in addition to national investment, private sources will invest a further $2 billion in building, industry, etc. The overall investment will thus reach $5 billion.[29]

On top of this heavy drain on the society's resources came the Lebanon war, variously estimated to cost from one to two million dollars a day, the total cost of which may have been as high as $5 billion from June 1982 until Israel's withdrawal was completed in mid-1985.

The Israeli budget is normally divided into three roughly equal portions allocated to defence, servicing the debt and general expenditures. Before June 1982 about half of the general budget was spent on the settlement programme; the other half on social services, welfare, education and health. But after the fighting began, defence took 46 per cent of the budget, taking this not from the settlement portion but from public programmes in Israel which were starved for funds. Economic dislocation caused by the Likud's political and military policies was aggravated by rocketing inflation brought on by the Government's economic policies. In 1977 there was a 34.6 per cent increase in the consumer price index, in 1978 a 50.3 per cent increase, in 1979 it was 77.8 per cent, in 1980, 132.6 per cent, in 1981, 101.3 per cent; in 1982 it jumped to 160–200 per cent, in 1983 to over 300 per cent and in 1984 to 444.9 per cent, falling to about 300 per cent in the first half of 1985 and to 43.4 per cent in the first half of 1986.[30]

The effect on the country of the collapsing economy was dramatic: between 1977 and 1982 the number of people living below the poverty line doubled from 250,000 to 500,000, representing 14.3 per cent of the population.[31] By the end of 1984 the Israeli unemployment rate — traditionally low — was 6 per cent of the workforce, 40 per cent of this unemployment occurring in the Oriental development towns. And there was a 50 per cent rise in an already high crime rate.

Between 1981 and 1983 the budget deficit doubled, from $2.2 billion to $4.2 billion and in 1984 a senior treasury adviser predicted that, without a reversal of the established trend, the total deficit would reach an annual sum of $8.6 billion in 1987, which would be added to the $6.3 billion for debt repayment, producing a deficit Israel would be unable to finance. By the end of 1987 the national external debt would reach $41.2 billion, amounting to a doubling of the debt within five years.[32] Although the economy was the first and most urgent priority of the national unity government, financial experts doubted the Government's ability to bring the situation under control before 1987.

Although the Likud's policies beggared Israel, this did not diminish the expectations of the annexationists who have always laid claim to an important portion of the budget for the territories and who would keep the defence budget at its high post-1967 level in order to finance the time-honoured Iron Wall strategy as well as the occupation. Annexation — accelerated or creeping — is an expensive endeavour. The peace front would offer Israel a different alternative, one in which part of the Land would be sacrificed in order to save the Soul of Israel.

Repartition of the Land

The scenario the peace front would write, which at present has little chance of being played, would involve the surrender by Israel of the territories to Arab sovereignty — amounting, in Zionist-messianic terms, to a *renunciation* of a part of the Land. From this single act all good things would flow: Israel would regain the special sentimental position it held in the Diaspora and among nations until 1967 when it became an alien occupier in territories inhabited by a defiant people. The IDF could cease to be an army of occupation — with all such a role entails in terms of the assumption of judicial, administrative and political powers — and return to its original role as a mobile, first-strike force. And it could be reduced to the level of a purely defensive force — which it has not been since the 1940s when the Haganah acquired the ability to create the state. The dangerous and anti-democratic partnership between the political and military establishments could be dissolved — preventing the chance of a reoccurence of a Sharon-type *putsch*. Israel's military expenditure could, consequently, be more than halved, and its soldiers required to serve fewer days in the reserves.

Peace would bring normalization, both external and internal. Israel would retain its Jewishness, safeguard its democracy and become a true spiritual centre for the Diaspora. Israel would develop trade and social ties with its neighbours and become less dependent on the US. A retreat from territorial messianism would reduce the influence of the religious establishment, and remove the threat Orthodoxy poses to the State. And this would strengthen Israel's relationship with the non-Orthodox Diaspora.

In 1982 Israel learned that the practice the late Nahum Goldman, President of the World Zionist Organization, called its 'policy of military superiority' and 'ruthless intimidation' [33] of the Arabs did not work. Peace was no nearer than it had been at the state's establishment and a substantial proportion of the population realized this. Such realization made the peace lobby, for the first time, a real force in Israeli politics. But because of the society's polarization into two cultures and because of the political deadlock, the peace front has had to turn to the Diaspora, and Israel's American ally, for assistance in the peace campaign. As the majority in Israel has come to accept that the Diaspora will not be in-gathered, and that its great pioneering days are over, it must also learn to accept that the Zionist dream of sovereignty over all of Eretz Yisrael can be no more than a dream.

Notes

1. The article cited on the Galilee district was published in *The Jerusalem Post*, 3 October 1984.

2. David Krivine's article appeared in *The Jerusalem Post International Edition*, 3-9 February 1985. The paper also published a selection of angry letters on 'Who is a Jew?' issue, particularly on the issue of the status of the Ethiopian immigrants.

3. Two key articles on the nature of Zionism are: by Dov Bar-Nir in *New Outlook*, March/April 1984; and an interview by Boaz Evron in *Hotam*, 26 September 1984.

4. Yosef Goell wrote on Gush Emunim in *The Jerusalem Post International Edition*, 22-27 May 1984; also Philip Jacobson in *The Times*, 10 July 1984.

5. Kahane was quoted by Glen Frankel in *The International Herald Tribune*, 13 August 1984.

6. Dani Rubinstein's article appeared in *Davar*, 27 July 1984.

7. Thomas L. Friedman in *The International Herald Tribune*, 31 May to 1 June 1986.

8. Christopher Walker's article appeared in *The Times*, 21 August 1984.

9. The quotation from the Karp Report is taken from an article by David Blundy and Hirsh Goodman in *The Sunday Times*, 3 June 1984.

10. The defender of the underground quoted was Rabbi Maurice Lamm of Los Angeles; from a letter published in *The International Herald Tribune*, 20 August 1984.

11. The Rabbinate's edicts were reported in *Ha'aretz*, 8 August 1982; the edict of the Sephardi Chief Rabbi appeared in the same paper on 24 June 1982.

12. The soldier at the front spoke to Robert Fisk of *The Times*, 17 June 1982.

13. Victor Shem-Tov's letter appeared in *Davar*, 14 October 1982.

14. Shevah Weiss also wrote in *Davar* on 3 October 1982.

15. Verbal violence was discussed by Eliahu Salpeter in *Ha'Aretz*, 12 October 1982.

16. Mrs David Landau was the eyewitness: She wrote about the incident in a letter to *The Jerusalem Post International Edition*, 3-9 October 1982.

17. *The Jerusalem Post*'s editorial on the 30th Zionist Congress appeared on 17 December 1982.

18. *The Jerusalem Post International Edition*, 2-8 March 1986.

19. Ibid.

20. A long report on Nazareth appeared in *The Jerusalem Post International Edition*, 4-10 December 1983.

21. Israel Shahak's article appeared in *Our Socialism*, Volume I, Number 6, November-December 1983.

22. Professor Harkabi is quoted from a letter he wrote for *Ha'aretz*, 11 May 1984.

23. An excellent analysis of the campaign is given in the 'Background' sheet of *Israel Press Briefs* published by the International Centre for Peace in the Middle

East, Number 26, July 1984.

24. Shifra Blass was quoted in *The Jerusalem Post International Edition*, 22-27 May 1984.

25. The July opinion survey was made by *Ha'aretz*, 27 July 1984.

26. Arie Lavie in *Ha'aretz*, 7 March 1986.

27. The federalist plan has been outlined in publications of the Jerusalem Centre for Public Affairs, one of which is *Shared Rule: The Only Realistic Option for Peace*, June 1983.

28. *The West Bank and Gaza, Data Base Project, Interim Report No. 1*, published by Meron Benvenisti, September 1982, Table 1a. For later figures published by Benvenisti, see Thomas L. Friedman in *The International Herald Tribune*, 11 February 1985.

29. The settlement plan was outlined by Israel Tomer in *Yedioth Aronoth*, 9 November 1983.

30. The inflation rate was taken from 'The Israeli Inflationary Experience', by Philip Ross, a *Jerusalem Letter* , 23 June 1982.

31. The report on poverty was published by the National Insurance Institute, 17 January 1984.

32. The economic crisis was described by Zvi Timor, the economic correspondent of *Al-Hamishmar*, in *New Outlook*, January 1984.

33. Goldman was quoted in an obituary editorial by *The Jerusalem Post International Edition*, 5-11 September 1982.

6. Can There be Peace in the Middle East?

Having determined that there is an influential and committed peace lobby in Israel, the question must be asked, Is there a peace option? For the Arabs, and the Palestinians, the price of peace is Israeli withdrawal from virtually all the territory occupied in 1967 according to the internationally accepted Resolution 242 of the United Nations Security Council. To answer this question one must pose another: Can the territories be handed back?

Meron Benvenisti, whose West Bank Data Project has surveyed and evaluated the extent of settlement and the physical infrastructure tying the territories to Israel, concluded that the process of ingestion was 'irreversible'. The inference to be drawn from this conclusion was that Israel could not and would not trade territory for peace and Israelis of goodwill had better content themselves with campaigning for civil rights for the Palestinians in the territories. But Tsaly Rechef, a leader of Peace Now, argues, 'In world history, processes which looked more irreversible were changed. Even if we had 100,000 to 200,000 Jews living in the West Bank . . . it would still be reversible.' [1]

First, because these Israelis would be among 800,000 Palestinians who, by sheer weight of numbers, must determine the demographic and social character of the region. Second, because, according to Stephen S. Rosenfeld of *The Washington Post*, '80 to 100 of the 150 settlements in the West Bank are flimsy affairs that could be taken down in an afternoon.' [2] And this was confirmed by Benvenisti who has said that 40 per cent of these settlements have 20 families or less. He has also stated that of all the settlements in the West Bank only the 15 around Jerusalem and north-east of Tel Aviv are viable and that most new settlers go to these rather than the others. Third, according to Benvenisti's 1986 report, [3] the pace of settlement slowed down in 1984–5, the number of settlers growing by only 9,400, about 6,000 fewer than during the previous year. And fourth, because of the 52,000 Israelis living in the West Bank only about 10 per cent were 'ideological settlers' whilst the overwhelming majority were merely residents attracted there by heavily subsidized housing. Such people would be prepared to go if compensated; indeed, many Israelis have bought into West Bank schemes in the hope that they would be compensated on a scale similar to that offered to the evacuees from Yamit. According to Benvenisti, there is still enough housing, either under construction or empty, to accommodate 2,000 Jewish families a year until available housing is filled, which would not be until 1986-7.

In the view of Ra'anan Weitz, who was head of the Jewish Agency's Settlement Department from 1962 until July 1984, the 'settlements' established by the Likud are 'empty balloons' which are not economically self-sufficient or socially coherent.[4] Concerning the Benvenisti estimate that 50 per cent of the land of the West Bank is now under Israeli control, Weitz argues that this so far amounts to 'facts on paper' only, in preparation for the next stage which is 'to create facts on the ground'. Weitz concludes, 'It works out, therefore, that all the territory that has changed by civilian day-by-day occupation consists of only 2 per cent of the West Bank territory.'[5]

Citizens' Rights Movement Knesset Member Yossi Sarid (the former Labour dove), in an interview,[6] viewed the Benvenisti report as a

negative contribution . . . the Likud wants to create the impression that in the West Bank unquestionable facts are created, and that what occurred is irreversible. Benvenisti is interested in creating this impression in the public opinion in Israel and especially abroad. [Indeed he was asked on the telephone, while this writer was present, if he would be prepared to testify to the Settlement Department of the Jewish Agency on the situation in the territories.] Thus the Likud received an unexpected service, which is invaluable, from an expert witness such as Benvenisti . . . In recent years there were global and regional political circumstances which aided the settlement effort of Gush Emunim and the Israeli government . . . there are several signs that this situation is about to change . . . In Sarid's opinion, we are at the end of the settlement season. The last seven years were, according to him, the good years for the settlers; now there will be five, or seven, bad years. 'The situation . . . of generosity . . . cannot continue' . . .

in the period of economic crisis that was precipitated by the Lebanon war. One further comment from Professor Mattityahu Peled, Knesset Member from the Progressive List for Peace: 'Benvenisti has one basic assumption which I do not accept. He thinks that the most important fact in the discussion of the solution of the Palestinian problem is the hundreds of tons of cement . . . in the West Bank.'

There is evidence that the Israeli economy would benefit from the return of the territories for reasons other than the redirecting of expenditure back across the Green Line. The occupation has produced serious structural problems in the economy — both long- and short-term. Two articles published in February 1984 in two differently-oriented Israeli newspapers described what had already happened and outlined how development was expected to proceed. The first article was on the impact of the occupation on employment. Dr Eliahu Borochov wrote:

One little noticed phenomenon that has emerged . . . over the past few years is the ongoing decline of Jewish males in the Labour force. In 1967, 71 per cent of Jewish males in Israel formed part of the labour market, either working or seeking work. By 1982, the figure had fallen to 63 per cent. This means that the number of working Jewish males has decreased by about 112,000. That is, had behavioural patterns remained as they were in 1967 . . . the [Jewish] work force would have stood at 846,000 instead of the actual 734,000. To see this development in its proper dimensions, we must bear in mind that the number of workers from the territories employed in Israel is estimated at 79,000 . . . One explanation for the phenomenon is . . . that [the Palestinian] workers replaced Jewish workers who left the labour market or never entered it, [and] that many types of employment and professions have become 'Arab work' — the kind of work no self-respecting Jew would engage in — or, more widespread still, permit his children to engage in. In many cases the influx of Arabs is accompanied by the worsening of working conditions and a decline in the prestige of a job.[7]

The Israelis replaced in the employment structure have been mainly unskilled Orientals, who comprise the most volatile element in the society.

The other problem concerns the overall imbalance in the economic structure and how it has been made worse by the development of the territories. This was described by Ra'anan Weitz: The Israeli economy is deformed because of the high proportion of people employed in the 'non-productive' services sector — 'the highest [proportion] in the world', and the low proportion employed in industry, 30 per cent as compared with 48 per cent in Italy, 43 per cent in Spain and 37 per cent in Portugal. This situation is exacerbated by the Jewish employment structure in the territories where '84 per cent . . . currently residing in the West Bank settlements is engaged in local services' and casual labour. A significant number are not even employed in the territories, but in Israel to which they must commute for their work. 'This imbalance . . . is an "economic deformity". It could be argued that the present situation is merely the beginning, and that the productive branches will develop only after a suitable service infrastructure has been established.' But according to the development plan for the region only '15 per cent [of its Jewish population] will work in industry, 2 per cent in agriculture, tourism and leisure and no less than 83 per cent in services and outside work also consisting largely of services.' Thus, Weitz expected that 'the economic deformity' would 'not only remain' but would be 'aggravated'.[8]

A poll published as long ago as May 1983[9] showed how the Israeli public viewed the occupation: 51 per cent of the respondents were for the return of most of the area, while 22 per cent were for annexation, and 17 per cent wanted to leave things as they were. West Bank correspondent Dani Rubenstein, writing just after the results of this poll were published,[10] explained why the settlers had lost the support of the majority. He pointed out that 'at a time of serious economic crisis' the settlers, no longer 'spartan, pioneerlike youngsters' but 'sated local councils, organizations, educational institutions, and development companies, rolling in money' kept crying out for more while social services, slum development projects, assistance for the elderly and education were starved for funds. He cited fraud in the selling of unbuilt houses or offering plots where none were available: '. . .there is no lack of scandals'. Settler violence had not helped their cause. 'And if that isn't enough . . . they are also (and perhaps mainly) involved in internal bickering.'

If the 'settlement season' had indeed come to an end as early as March 1983, then it should have been a simple task for the peace front to explode the 'irreversibility theory'. But people tend to cling to familiar ideas long after such ideas become obsolete. Thus, according to Avraham Burg, it took the Israeli public three years to accept the lessons of the 1973 combined Arab attack on Israel. And even then the society did not draw the important conclusions it should have from the failure of the civil-military echelon: nothing was done to institute civilian checks on the military or to separate the functions of the two establishments. Such a separation would have made it impossible, in 1982, for Sharon to launch a war without the full, and prior, approval of the Cabinet. Thus, the irreversibility theory persists because of the obstinate credulity (and wishful thinking) of the Israeli public, and of the people abroad who do not know better. The danger of irreversibility does not lie in the West Bank countryside but in the minds of men.

And this is particularly true in the case of the two areas where the Israelis have most firmly established their physical presence, both being key to an Arab-Israeli peace. The first — and of prime importance — is Greater Jerusalem, where Israel has settled over 100,000 people within the expanded municipal limits. There the obstacle would be Israel's refusal to give up the eastern, Arab portion of the city, ruled by Jordan from 1948 until its capture and annexation by Israel in 1967. Israel's attitude was defined by Defence Minister Moshe Dayan on 7 June 1967, at the Wailing Wall after the Israeli seizure of the city: 'We have returned to our holiest places. We have returned never to be parted from them again.' This doctrine was reinforced and formalized by the prompt annexation of East Jerusalem. Since its occupation the Israelis have enclosed the city within a wall of high-rise apartment blocks, built of stone along the spare lines of crusader castles, with small windows set deeply into the walls: the IDF's fortified positions in case of a third battle for the city. The Arabs are adamant that there can be no peace without Arab sovereignty returning to both the Old City within the walls and the modern Palestinian town to the east. The plan of Jerusalem's Israeli Mayor Teddy Kollek for a unified municipality with separate Israeli and Palestinian boroughs could be adapted to work under divided sovereignty, if there was an Israeli consensus favouring such a compromise — which is yet a long way off. So far only the more radical elements in the peace front openly speak of the need for compromise on Jerusalem. Peace Now gives priority to the territories because their return is a much less emotive issue than Jerusalem.

The second area is the Syrian Golan Heights which Israel conquered, claimed and annexed for 'security reasons'. Some 8,000 Jewish settlers have been introduced into the region, which has a population of 15,000 Syrian Druze, although before 1967 the population was over 100,000. In spite of the fact that modern weapons technology has made obsolete Israel's claims that it must retain the Heights for 'security reasons', the Government would be reluctant to relinquish its hold on the Golan because of a mental fixation that Syria could dominate the Galilee from the Heights.

The Dayan plan for the integration of the territories which has been the basis of both Labour and Likud policies has two objectives: first, to make

Israel's presence irreversible through settlement and, second, to integrate the area into the Israeli economy and tie it to Israel's infrastructure of roads, electricity grids and water systems so that separation would become physically impossible. Security formed a part of this policy as well: this was defined in a phrase used by Meron Benvenisti in an interview in *Al-Hamishmar* in December 1983, '. . . we can sit on the faucet and rule them',[11] referring to a practice of placing the control of the water supply to every Palestinian town or village connected to the Israeli system in Israeli hands. (A practice inaugurated by Ben Gurion to have certain means to control the Palestinians remaining inside the Jewish state after the 1948-9 war). Israeli policies were precisely designed to prevent the building of an independent Palestinian economic infrastructure. And they have been profitable policies, because Palestinians have not been permitted to establish industrial enterprises which would compete with Israeli industry or, lately, even to grow the same crops. Israel exports to the West Bank finished products worth more than $800 million a year.

A study published in 1984 by Benvenisti's West Bank Data Base Project[12] showed that the $6.6 million allocated by the US Government for West Bank development from 1977 to 1983 was not used for that purpose but was either invested in public works and services, for which Israel was supposed to be responsible, or used to subsidize the administration, including its pacification programmes. The Military Administration exercised control over the projects through vetting procedures, for example by putting projects involving the importation of agricultural and industrial machinery into protracted administrative limbo by simply denying approval. The objective was to restrict local employment opportunities for Palestinians, forcing them to emigrate.

According to a survey made by the research department of the Bank of Israel a total freeze clamped down on economic development in the West Bank in 1983. This reflected the economic crisis in Israel, but because of the lower base due to Israel's restrictive policies, the recession in the West Bank was more severe than in Israel, with unemployment at its highest level ever and few employment opportunities for Palestinians in the oil-producing Gulf states due to the economic crisis there. In an attempt to ameliorate the situation US Secretary of State George Shultz called for improvement of the 'quality of life' in the territories, and a committee of American Jews and Arab personalities was established to promote such development projects as a Palestinian bank in Nablus (refused permission by Israel since 1967). The intention behind this approach was to defuse political tension by raising the standard of living of the Palestinian population. But before this joint effort got beyond the planning stage it was assailed by Gush Emunim and the Tehiya Party and the more militant element in Herut for whom, in the words of Dani Rubinstein, 'every factory, every road and Arab house are . . . the infrastructure of the Palestinian state.'[13] Because the Israeli Government is susceptible to pressure from these quarters there is little expectation that independent development would be allowed in the territories and every expectation that the present integration-suppression programme would make it all the more difficult to extricate the territories from the occupation. But the Palestinians have repeatedly stated that they would opt for separation, if given the opportunity, whatever the cost.

It is clear that neither settlement nor integration has made Israeli rule over the territories irreversible and because the Arabs insist on the return of territory for peace, a peace option does, in principle, exist. What are the prospects?

As a result of the Likud's messianic politics a political centre has emerged in Israel for the first time, and this centre has distanced itself from traditional Labour policy, rejected the Revisionist-messianic programme and allied itself with Israel's peace front which, though it contains several political parties, remains an extra-parliamentary pressure group. But the peace front is not solid: its constituents differ widely on what and how much territory should be traded for peace, the status of Jerusalem, the Palestinian future. However, the extremism of the messianic camp, its increasing use of violence, has made the peace front coalesce and propelled it towards an agreed programme.

What is required is no less than a change in the course of 100 years of Zionist history, not a tactical pause in the extension of Jewish sovereignty over all of Eretz Yisrael. To achieve this the peace front has to muster the will-power to reject the primary Zionist goal and reverse the direction of the Zionist endeavour. It is not enough for the peace front simply to allow a settlement freeze to happen because Israel may be in the throes of a short-term economic crisis; it must take advantage of the situation to obtain a decision from the Government that settlement activity will not be resumed.

Avraham Burg believes that the Lebanese war gave Israel the 'chance for a chance' to make the necessary reassessment, not more than that. This reassessment must not be motivated by negative forces but by positive ones, he says: if the motivation is negative — rejection of the Likud and its policies — the reassessment will not succeed. A 'revolution' is needed, he argues, 'to change the system'. Burg, himself an observant Jew, believes there must be clear separation between Church and State. The peace front needs to move into the institutions of the State and reshape them from within, as the Labour Zionists moved into and took over the Zionist Organization in the twenties.

There has been one important example of a dovish programme being adopted by Israeli institutions: a pilot scheme has been initiated for the revision of school curricula in order that the image of the Arabs projected to Israeli children is less hostile and more understanding. Prepared by the Van Leer Jerusalem Institute the project was taken up by the Ministry of Education while the Likud was still in power. Alouph Hareven, who is in charge of the education project, summed up what he hopes will be accomplished: 'Nations change; their perceptions of reality and of themselves change; the course of history changes.'[14] But what is needed is not only a change in the attitude towards the Arabs, and the Palestinians, but also a change in the attitudes held by the Israelis about themselves, about what they have done and what they can achieve.

Ezer Weizman, a former Defence Minister and Minister without Portfolio in the 1984 national unity government, summed up Israel's difficulty in confronting its future:

> evidently we have to undergo some sort of psychological transformation before we can believe in the peace [process] and move ahead. We of the military raised an entire generation to be fighters. The generations to come will have to educate the people of Israel, in an intelligent and rational manner, to believe in the necessity of peace agreements between us and the Arabs. That's a lot harder than doing battle. On the battlefield . . . you get immediate results. When it comes to peace, things are more vague. [15]

Even if the peace front were to secure the support of a majority of Israelis for a peace plan acceptable to the Arabs, the politico-military establishment would not permit the will of the people to prevail. It would not be in its interest as the power-holding class to acquiesce in a peaceful settlement, particularly because so many of the politicians are either ex-IDF or ex-Defence Ministry or ex-intelligence — Navon, Peres, Shamir and Rabin, to name the topmost echelon. Ezer Weizman knows full well that the military would be the last State institution to promote the demilitarization of the society it has so completely militarized. Peace would force the military from its partnership position in the State structure and force out of office the independence generation of politicians who think only in terms of security and messianic conquest.

Although refusal to negotiate peace has been a feature of Israeli policy since the founding of the state, the Israeli public was educated to the idea that Israel could never have peace because of the atavistic hostility of the Arabs. The visit of Egypt's President Anwar Sadat to Jerusalem showed the Israelis for the first time that peace was attainable. But then the Camp David Accords which were a result of Sadat's initiative did not produce the regional peace hoped for or the normalization of Israel's status *vis à vis* the Arabs which the Israelis expected. Prime Minister Menachem Begin had no intention of concluding a true peace with Egypt which would include real self-determination for the Palestinians in the occupied territories. Begin's objective was to remove Egypt as a confrontation state and he was prepared to pay Sadat's price, the return of Sinai. Thus Camp David was never more than a partial, even a false peace which is why its normalization provisions have only been implemented in a token fashion and why, after the Israeli invasion of Lebanon in 1982, it became a 'cold peace', an absence of belligerency solely.

The Israeli establishment never liked the Israeli–PLO ceasefire along the Lebanese frontier mediated by US envoy Philip Habib in July 1981 because it circumscribed Israel's military activities in southern Lebanon. But Israel could not but do the bidding of its powerful ally and it could not afford to be seen as the aggressive party. While abiding by the ceasefire the Begin government made its preparations for the war the Israeli people did not want, the war which did not receive the approval of the Cabinet until after it had been launched with airstrikes on Beirut and the south on 4 June.

The mass demonstrations against the war and the occupation of Lebanon during 1982 and 1983–4 did not force the Government to pull back or pull out, which it did only after the IDF demanded the evacuation of the Chouf in September 1983 and the withdrawal from most of southern Lebanon 18 months later. The IDF imposed its will on the politicians because it had suffered too many casualties in Lebanon and too serious a deterioration of morale.

In November 1984 PLO Chairman Yasser Arafat secured the approval of the Palestine National Council to conclude an agreement with King Hussein to negotiate with Israel on the basis of an exchange of peace for the territory occupied in 1967. For the PLO this was an unprecedented peace initiative and a major policy shift towards compromise. Moreover, the PLO undertook to restrict the exercise of self-determination for the Palestinian people, agreeing to the establishment of a confederation with Jordan instead of the independent Palestinian state the majority of Palestinians want. In February 1985 the King and Arafat agreed on a joint programme and launched a cooperative peace initiative. But this came to nothing because Israel refused to consider it, and the US followed suit. This made the King renounce cooperation with the PLO in February 1986. During that critical year Prime Minister Peres proclaimed an alternative plan based on the shared rule concept of the 'federalists' — which the Palestinians in the territories see as a disguised version of the 'not-one-inch' programme promoted by the most militant section of the Israeli population.

According to an opinion poll conducted in April 1986 the Israeli public is not as reluctant as its Government to negotiate with the dreaded PLO. Indeed, the sample polled was equally divided between those who favoured negotiations with the PLO, if it recognized Israel and renounced terrorism, and those who opposed. Negotiations with the moderate PLO were favoured by 60 per cent of second-generation sabras, 53 per cent of European immigrants and their children and 45 per cent of Oriental Jews and their children. Thirty-one per cent of those who identified themselves as Orthodox would agree to talks, 51 per cent of those who said they were 'traditional' (observant) and 54 per cent of those who said they were non-observant (secular); 40 per cent of Likud supporters surveyed would agree and 66 per cent of Alignment supporters.

This poll also exposed the public's view of the military: 53 per cent of those questioned believed that the military, to quote *The Jerusalem Post*, 'used criteria other than the merit of a situation in making a decision', that priority was given to 'personal and organizational factors'.[16] This erosion of the popular image of the IDF — which began in 1973 — has made that State structure all the more dangerous because it is constantly trying to recoup its lost prestige. Since 1982, in particular, the IDF has been trying to shed its image as the 'IDF of Lebanon'.

Since early in 1986 the Israeli press has been predicting that Israel would launch a war against Syria before the year was out.[17] Both Labour and Likud have good internal political reasons for conducting a short, sharp war against Syria. A Labour-led war would be more popular than one waged by the Likud because Labour's motives are not as suspect as those of the Likud: the public would be more likely to believe that Labour would fight a defensive war while a Likud-led war would be considered messianic and expansionist. A successful military campaign would enable Peres to call elections and perhaps improve his party's position in the Knesset enough to form a new narrow-based government. Such a war, whether conducted by Labour or Likud, would also ensure that Yitzak Shamir, under challenge from David Levy and Ariel Sharon, would retain the leadership of the Likud. A successful Likud-led campaign could wipe from the public mind the failures of 1978 (the Litani Operation) and 1982.

Before fighting could begin, however, the Government had to prepare public opinion with a carefully orchestrated publicity campaign — particularly since only one-third anticipated an imminent war, meaning only that one-third accepted the fact that a war with Syria was unavoidable.[18] The Peres government operated on two tracks: on the one hand, it tried to show itself reluctant to take action and that it was prepared to be patient with Israel's troublesome neighbour, and on the other, it had to develop enough tension within the society to make the resort to war acceptable. In May the habitually cautious Peres was compelled to rebuke, obliquely, his Defence Minister, Yitzak Rabin, who, during a visit to Washington, informed American officials of Israel's intention to initiate military action against Syria because of Syrian support for 'International terrorism'. Rabin's 'anti-Syrian ardour', wrote Peretz Kidron, 'borders on a life-long obsession'.[19] As Commander-in-Chief in 1967 he bore the major responsibility for creating the tension along the Syrian border that enabled Israel to go to war in June. Peres countered Rabin's aggressive posturing by wheeling in the armed forces commander, among others, to reassure the Israeli people. Peres evidently convinced Rabin that his revelations had been previous and got him to moderate his approach. Rabin then declared that Israel had 'no interest in a military confrontation with Syria' and expressed the opinion that Syria was 'not now eager to go to war'. The official communiqué issued after a Cabinet meeting on 11 May said that Israel would 'do everything in its power to avoid war' with Syria, but left Israel's options open by stating that the world must 'do everything necessary' to put an end to Syrian sponsorship of 'terrorism'.

The aim of the war would be 'to destroy Syria', asserted Samuel Segev,[20] the distinguished military correspondent of *Ma'ariv*. Since the abrogation of the US-sponsored Lebanon–Israel agreement, Syria has been seen by Israel, and the US, as the key political operator in the region, able, at least, to prevent separate deals between various Arab regimes and Israel — which is what the US and Israel seek to achieve. Thus the regime of Hafez Al-Assad is seen as the major obstacle in the way of arrangements which would give Israel 'peace for peace' rather than 'peace for territory' which has been the Arab demand. Israel's other reasons for attacking Syria are important but secondary: Syria has improved and re-equipped its armed forces since 1982, and Peres, as the father of the concept of 'preventive war', would like to prevent Syria from making further improvements, particularly the development of offensive capacity. Israel wants to drive Syria out of Lebanon. Israel is irritated by the

Soviet ground-to-air missiles installed by Syria in the Bekaa Valley as a first line of defence against Israeli air attacks on Damascus. Israel would like to destroy Syria's recently fortified defensive positions also in the Bekaa and to raze the pro-Syrian Palestinian and Lebanese Shia Muslim militia training camps there because they provide fighters for the running battle against the IDF and its surrogate South Lebanon Army in the Israeli security zone north of the frontier.

To achieve a climate propitious for launching a punitive action, Israel, in January, shot down over Lebanon two Syrian fighter planes which fell in Syrian territory and, in February, the Israeli airforce intercepted and force-landed in northern Israel a Libyan executive jet which was carrying several high-ranking members of the Syrian regime. The reason given for this provocative act was that the Libyan plane was carrying Palestinian 'terrorist' leaders back to Damascus after a 'terrorist conference' in Tripoli. The authoritative P. Sever, writing in *Al-Hamishmar,* [21] dismissed this excuse and stated that the Israeli Government intended to hijack those very Syrian personages as a strong provocation. Israel duly apologized for both incidents: Sever said that this method of provocation-by-mistake had been adopted by Israel to heighten tension in preparation for the attack.

In January–February Israel, joined by the US, launched a full-scale propaganda campaign, first, against Syria for what Israel construed to be belligerent declarations by President Assad, then, against Syria and Libya, for their alleged complicity in terrorist incidents. Israel claimed a Syrian connection with a bombing attempt made on an El Al airliner in London in April. Syria was also alleged to bear responsibility for attacks at Rome and Vienna airports on 27 December 1985, and was also allegedly involved in the Berlin disco bombing in early April which gave the US a pretext to launch airstrikes against Libya, initially held responsible for the incident.

The Israeli Government has economic as well as political reasons for fighting a brief war with Syria. [22] A war would divert attention from the general débâcle which the Government's anti-inflationary policy has produced. A war would enable the armaments industry to sell to the IDF the 40 per cent of its production it failed to export because of the falling off of this trade. Such sales would both save the various firms which have a heavy burden of debt and preserve the jobs of the workers in this key 'security' sector of the economy. A war would provide IDF employment for workers otherwise unemployed.

According to Levy Morav, writing in *Al-Hamishmar,* [23] the campaign would be partially financed by the US, which wants to see the Soviet Union's closest Arab ally beaten and disgraced, and partially by the money saved from the cuts in subsidies on basic foodstuffs (turning butter into guns) and from the reduction of wages under the Government's economic programme. Finally a war would enable the Government to raise taxes both to pay for the campaign while it lasted and to restore to the IDF the sums cut from its budget.

Three months after the publicity campaign began, most of the Israeli press spoke of the war with Syria as one 'unavoidable fact', as did such opponents of belligerent activity as the Citizens' Rights Movement's chief dove, Yossi Sarid. *Al-Hamishmar* and *Monatin* were the only two papers which warned against the war and against the attitude of expectation which would make war possible. The atmosphere in Israel was comparable to that prevailing in the run-up to the Lebanon war. It was clear that the people of Israel were not permitted to make peace because their rulers must make war. Though the popular will may act as a temporary brake, which could delay war, it cannot eliminate the inevitable lashing-out. As a former head of Military Intelligence said in March 1986: 'We are in the process of the countdown to the next war.'[24]

Notes

1. Tsaly Reshef was quoted in an article by Trudy Rubin in *The Christian Science Monitor*, 15 August 1983.

2. The Rosenfeld article appeared in *The International Herald Tribune*, 27 February 1984.

3. For Benvenisti's latest figures see *The Jerusalem Post International Edition*, 8 February 1986, and *1986 Report: Demographic, economic, legal, social developments in the West Bank* (West Bank Data Base Project, 1986).

4. Rena'an Weitz's article appeared in *Ha'aretz*, 24 April 1985.

5. The article cited appeared in *The Jerusalem Post International Edition*, 15-21 July 1984, on the occasion of Weitz's retirement. The longer quotations are from his April 1985 *Ha'aretz* article.

6. Aryeh Dayan interviewed Sarid and Peled in *Koteret Rachit*, 14 and 21 March 1984.

7. Borochov's article appeared in *Ma'ariv*, 4 February 1984.

8. Weitz's article appeared in *Ha'aretz*, 5 February 1984.

9. The poll appeared in *Davar*, 13 May 1983.

10. Dani Rubinstein's article was in *Davar*, 13 March 1983.

11. Benvenisti's interview by Dalya Shikhori was in *Al-Hamishmar*, December 1984.

12. Benvenisti's report was entitled 'U.S. Funded Projects in the West Bank and Gaza (1977-1983)', Working Paper No. 13. An account of the report appeared in *The Jerusalem Post*, 6 April 1984.

13. Dani Rubinstein in *Davar*, 19 November 1984.

14. Alouph Hareven was quoted in *The Jerusalem Post*, 13 July 1982.

15. Weizman was interviewed by Eitan Haber in *Yedioth Ahronoth*, 2 November 1984.

16. *The Jerusalem Post International Edition*, 12 April 1986.

17. See Reuven Padatsur in *Ha'aretz*, 4 March 1986.

18. The *Ha'aretz* poll was mentioned in *Middle East International* of 16 May 1986. The issue of this publication of 4 April 1986 also has material on Israel's intentions towards Syria.

19. Peretz Kidron was writing in *Middle East International*, 16 May 1986.

20. The date of Segev's article was 2 April 1986.

21. Sever's piece appeared on 6 February 1986.

22. For articles on the economic reasons see Shlomo Frankel in *Hadashot*, 7

March 1986; Arie Lavie in *Ha'aretz*, 7 March 1986; Alex Fishman in *Al-Hamishmar* of 25 February 1986.

23. The article, entitled 'Good, Short, Strong and Elegant' was published on 18 March 1986.

24. The head of Military Intelligence quoted was Shlomo Gavish in *Hadashot*, 6 March 1986.

CHART OF THE ISRAELI POLITICAL SCENE

This is far from being a complete chart of the Israeli political scene. It is meant to show where the parties and groupings mentioned in this book stand in the political spectrum.

SPIRITUAL

PARTIES	HADASH Democratic Front for Peace and Equality 4 Knesset seats	PROGRESSIVE LIST FOR PEACE Matti Peled 2 Knesset seats	MAPAM Left Labour 6 Knesset seats	RATZ Citizens' Rights Movement 5 Knesset seats
PROGRAMMES	Two-state solution based on Resolution 242 and Brezhnev Plan Negotiations with PLO	Two-state solution Negotiations with PLO	Land for peace and Jordanian option Against dismantling settlements Negotiations with PLO	Jordanian federation solution with "security arrangements" No negotiations with PLO

ORGANIZATIONS

Party Affiliated

MATZPEN and its factions		Israeli Council for Israeli Palestine Peace	
NATUREI KARTA Ultra-orthodox Anti-Zionist	Committee Against the War in Lebanon	Committee for Israeli Palestinian Dialogue (Oriental)	
Committee for Just Peace in the Middle East		Kibbutz Artzi	
Democratic Women and other Rakah communist affiliations	Yesh Gvul & Ad Kan	Hashomer Hatzair	
	Women against the Invasion of Lebanon (the Occupation) – Tel Aviv		
	Women against the War – Jerusalem		

Student

▓▓▓▓▓▓▓▓▓▓ CAMPUS ▓▓▓▓▓▓▓▓▓▓   OMETZ ▓▓▓▓▓▓▓▓▓▓

Rights

League for Human and Civil Rights	Beersheba Branch of Association for Civil Rights in Israel		Civil rights Group – Ratz
Prisoners Friends Association			

EDUCATION & DIALOGUE

	NEVE SHALOM Partnership		INTERNATIONAL CENTRE
			Van Leer Institute Educa
			RESHET
			Interns for Peace
			Education for Peace

DEMOCRATIC SOCIALIST

SHINUI Change Party	MAPAI Labour	OMETZ-TELEM	YAHAD Ezer Weizman
3 Knesset seats	36 Knesset seats	1 Knesset seat	3 Knesset seats
Jordanian federation solution	Jordanian option – no Palestinian state	Jordanian option – no Palestinian state	Opportunist
No negotiations with PLO	No negotiations with PLO	No negotiations with PLO	

▓▓▓▓▓▓▓ P E A C E N O W ▓▓▓			
Parents against Silence			
Mothers against Silence			
DI! (Enough)			
Way to Peace			
United Kibbutz Movement			
OFEK ▓▓▓▓▓▓▓▓▓▓▓▓▓▓▓▓▓▓▓▓▓▓▓▓▓			
	Association for Civil Rights in Israel		
	New Israel Fund (A. Burg)		

ACE IN THE MIDDLE EAST ▓▓

ogramme ▓▓▓

Institute for Education for Coexistence between Jews and Arabs

Gesher (Bridge)

Beit Hagefen

Ulpan Akiva

Secular

LIKUD Herut, La'am and Liberals	TAMI Oriental Tradition Party	TEHIYA Ultra-nationalist	NATIONAL RELIGIOUS PARTY
41 Knesset seats –	1 Knesset seat	5 Knesset seats	4 Knesset seats
Eretz Yisrael ideological focus	Eretz Yisrael ideological focus	Eretz Yisrael 'not-one-inch' approach	Eretz Yisrael ideological focus
Autonomy for Palestinians			
No negotiations with PLO	No negotiations with PLO	No negotiations with PLO	No negotiations with PLO

▓▓▓▓▓▓▓▓▓▓▓▓▓▓▓▓▓▓▓▓▓▓▓▓▓▓▓▓▓ LAND OF ISRAEL

Betar
(Youth Herut)

▓▓▓▓▓▓▓▓▓▓▓▓▓▓▓▓

Youth for Israel

East for Peace
(Oriental)

Gesher (Bridge)

Ulpan Akiva

Religious

AGUDAT YISRAEL Ultra-orthodox Party	SHAS Oriental Torah Guardians	MORASHA Religious ultra-nationalist	KACH Religious ultra-nationalist Rabbi M. Kahane	
2 Knesset seats	4 Knesset seats	2 Knesset seats	1 Knesset seat	**PARTIES**
Eretz Yisrael ideological focus	Eretz Yisrael ideological focus	Eretz Yisrael 'not-one-inch' approach	Eretz Yisrael drive-the-Palestinians-out approach	**PROGRAMMES**
No negotiations with PLO	No negotiations with PLO	No negotiations with PLO	No negotiations with PLO	
MOVEMENT ▬▬▬▬▬▬▬▬▬▬▬▬▬▬▬▬▬▬▬				
GUSH EMUNIM ▬▬▬▬▬▬▬▬▬▬				
Netivot Shalom		Temple Mount Faithful		**ORGANIZATIONS** Party Affiliated
Oz VeShalom			Terror Against Terror	
	KASTEL (Hebrew University)			Student
	MASSADA (Bar Ilan University)			
				Rights
Bit Hillel – Hebrew University Interfaith Association				**EDUCATION & DIALOGUE**
Martin Buber Centre			Partially based on material provided by Jan and Samir Abu Shakra of the Arab Studies Society, Jerusalem	

Index